ANTONIN ARTAUD

POET WITHOUT WORDS

by Naomi Greene

INTRODUCTION BY
Janet Flanner

SIMON AND SCHUSTER
New York

FIRST PRINTING

SBN 671–20721–0 (TRADE)
SBN 671–20722–9 (CLARION)
LIBRARY OF CONGRESS CATALOG CARD NUMBER: 74–130476
DESIGNED BY IRVING PERKINS
MANUFACTURED IN THE UNITED STATES OF AMERICA

To my parents

I would like to express my gratitude to Michel Beaujour, Thomas Bishop and Paule Thévenin for the help and understanding they have shown me in the preparation of this book.

CONTENTS

INTRODUCTION

Contemporary life has finally caught up with Antonin Artaud, twenty years after his death, in 1948, aged fifty-two. Nine of his years he had spent in lunatic asylums. An erudite, melancholy French esthete, of extraordinary, if alarmingly morose, facial beauty, and early magnetized by the theater, he became the creator of what is now internationally known as the Theater of Cruelty, as his reaction against bourgeois Parisian theatrical realism, and as an outlet for his philosophic horror of the contemporary Western World, which he declared was actuated only by "violence and aggression." In his egotism and imbalance, recognizing as realities only his own truths, he developed, outside the shape of normal society—and in maturity, in his twenties—creative gifts so isolated that he became, within his limits, one of the so-called *maudits,* or infernal creators, in French poetic thinking, of whom the last great disturbing figures had been Baudelaire and Rimbaud.

French theater experts today declare that Artaud has been a dominantly important seminal influence on the French avant-garde stage, on its directors, and, above all, on its writers, such as the Irish author Beckett, who writes in French and wrote the opening, baffling masterpiece of subtle cruelty called *Waiting for Godot.* In the same Paris school have been the prolific Rumanian playwriter Eugène Ionesco and the minor writers Adamov and Audiberti. The latest recruit is the Spaniard Arrabal, whose *Cemetery of Automobiles,* the Paris *succès d'estime* of 1968, developed the Artaud idea of the concrete presentation by including cacophony and

9

cruelly loud noise as the most audible part of the theme. Artaud probably had little or no influence on the plays of the French theater revolutionary Jean Genet, since it seems likely that Genet owes nothing to anybody, having always been complete on his own terrible scale. Theater directors who, in their productions, have best carried out the aims of Artaud—which, it must be understood, may have little to do with the text itself but furnish, in the manner of the presentation, a certain atmosphere of creative cruel anguish that amounts to interpretation—have been Jean-Louis Barrault, when he was manager of the Odéon, the producer Jean Vilar, and, above all, in the sense of complete emotional suffering, which is inflicted as a catalyst on the spectators, the director Roger Blin. The most talked-of play in Paris in June of 1969 was a perfect Artaud example directed by Blin. It was played in the tiny Théâtre de Poche in Montparnasse, which seats perhaps a hundred spectators and is down a little medieval alley. The play was called *Les Nonnes (The Nuns)*, was written by a Cuban, Eduardo Manet, and dealt with the terrors of a nineteenth-century revolt of Haitian slaves, in which the so-called nuns were cheroot-smoking, murderous bandits disguised as Sisters of Charity. By its brutal shocks it belonged to what used to be called in Paris Grand Guignol theater—in its heyday very popular with the French—but by its interpretative implications it belonged to today's Theater of Cruelty.

I first heard of Artaud in Paris back in the early 1920's, when he became a member of the newly founded Surrealist movement, in the wing dominated by the novelist Aragon, the poet Eluard, and the painter Masson. Another initial member was the late writer Pierre de Massot, a close friend of mine and as close a friend to Artaud as Artaud permitted, for it was almost impossible for him to be interested in human relationships. Those whom Artaud liked he could, and sometimes would, talk to brilliantly, but by nature he was *un solitaire*.

The minor intellectuals on the Paris Left Bank who used to know Artaud are now all dead. His personal traces today lie in his essays or in the Surrealist manifestoes that he wrote for Breton. I once went with de Massot to see Artaud act, in some small part, as a member of the Dullin avant-garde-theater troupe. He had a thin, sarcastic bony face, a deep voice that sounded as if he were deaf it was so unmodulated, his stage presence non-existent. He seemed to lack physical talent because of his conviction (de Massot explained to me) that any physical imitation of reality in presenting a character would have seemed bogus to him. His ideas of acting were anti-thespian. It thus seemed strange that he had elected to be an actor at all—the most susceptible position in the entire theater hierarchy and the most easily criticized, where the professional can be tortured with the greatest facility by lack of appreciation, always uppermost in Artaud's reactions, since he was a creature of hypersensitive pride and punctilio. I never saw any of the seventeen performances of his play adaptation of *The Cenci;* it was reportedly a fiasco. It was apparently even untrue to his own extraordinary theories of audience participation and the great cruel power of violence, which both ally him posthumously to the theater and to the world and to the people of today. In his life Artaud was an embittered failure, but since his death his theories on cruelty have, in part, enjoyed the popular success he never knew.

JANET FLANNER

KEY TO ABBREVIATIONS
OF ARTAUD'S WORK

I–VII   Volumes I–VII of the Gallimard edition of Artaud's collected works

C   *Lettre contre la Cabbale (Letter against the Cabala)*—No pagination

CE   *"Chiote à l'esprit"* ("Shit to the mind")

CG   *Ci-gît, précédé de la culture indienne (Here lies, preceded by Indian culture)*—No pagination

EV   *"Il fallait d'abord avoir envie de vivre"* ("You have to begin with a will to live")

F   *"Fragmentations"*

JD   *Pour en finir avec le jugement de dieu (To end god's judgment)*

JL   *"Je hais et abjecte en lâche"* ("I hate and denounce as a coward")

LL   *"Lettre sur Lautréamont"* ("Letter on Lautréamont")

LS   *"Là où j'en suis"* ("Here where I stand")

M   *México*

MM   *"Les malades et les médecins"* ("Patients and Doctors")

Momo   *Artaud le Momo*

PL   *"Lettre à Pierre Loeb"* ("Letter to Pierre Loeb")

R   *Lettres de Rodez (Letters from Rodez)*

SR   *Supplément aux Lettres de Rodez suivi de Coleridge le traître (Supplement to the Letters from Rodez, followed by Coleridge the Traitor)*

T   *Les Tarahumaras*

VG   *Van Gogh, le suicidé de la société (Van Gogh: The Man Suicided by Society)*

84   Issue No. 5–6 of the magazine entitled *84*

I

THE
MAN

Antonin Artaud is on his way to becoming one of the most discussed and least known writers of our generation. For a number of years after his death in 1948 the story of his life generated far more interest than did his work. This is hardly surprising since, throughout his life, Artaud, voluntarily or not, played to perfection the role of the misunderstood and tortured poet. His addiction to drugs, his apparent madness, his utter renunciation of Western culture, have exercised an irresistible attraction for young writers and thinkers, perhaps more so in the United States (where alienation has found fertile soil) than in his native France. Artaud personified alienation in its ultimate form; his insanity may be regarded as the final step in a progressive withdrawal from society. Fascinated by the myth of the man's personality, only a relatively few people are aware of the biographical facts concerning Artaud.[1]

The poet–playwright–actor was born in Marseilles on September 4, 1896, of a French father and a mother of Greek origin. As a child he learned several languages, for the household included an Italian governess, and his Greek grandmother, to whom he was very attached, spent much time with her grandson. His relationship with his mother was, from childhood, stormy and emotional. Of his father he saw relatively little. The latter's determination that his son take over his prosperous ship-fitting business may be partially responsible for Artaud's animosity toward him. Years later Artaud was to confess that "until I was 27 I lived with an obscure hatred of fathers, of my own father—until the day I saw him die. Then, this inhuman severity which I felt he had always exerted against me gave way. Another being came out of this body. And, for the first time in my life, this father held out his arms to me." (T, 176–177)

Illness, a constant companion to Artaud throughout his life, struck early. At five he suffered a near-fatal attack of meningitis. This disease occurred at a particularly trying time in the home. His mother had just lost a three-day-old baby and she turned, in grief and desolation, to her small and frail five-year-old. She apparently welcomed, and encouraged, her son's unhealthy tendency to depend greatly upon her. For his part, Artaud knew instinctively how to use his illness to manipulate his mother for the usual childish ends. Although it is highly conceivable that Artaud's early illness may have been the cause of his subsequent nervous disorders, there seems to be no way of ascertaining this medically. Nor, indeed, has the precise nature of these later disorders, accompanied as they were by pain so intense as to drive Artaud to the use of drugs, been explained by medical science. Even as a child, Artaud was desperately aware of the complexity of his physical and psychological problems: "Ever since my earliest childhood (6–8 years old), I have noticed these periods of stuttering and horrible physical contraction of my facial nerves and tongue which came after periods of calm and perfect ease. All of this was complicated by corresponding psychic problems that only appeared quite openly when I was about 19." (I, 312)

Photographs of Artaud as an adolescent reveal him to have been thin and extremely sensitive-looking, with deep, haunting eyes. His outward sensitivity was accompanied by an inner desire to write. At fourteen, Artaud started a little magazine, romantically using "Louis des Attides" as a nom de plume. A few years later, in 1915, only nineteen but already familiar with the tortures of depression and intense headaches, Artaud destroyed all his manuscripts and gave his books to friends. His worried parents decided to send him to the first of what was to be a long series of nursing homes. The following year, having seemingly regained his health, he was drafted into military service. In less than a year, however, his influential father obtained his release and he was discharged—for "sleepwalking," as he humorously told his friends.

Shortly after his release from the Army, Artaud was assailed by deep mystical longings and would spend days in prayer. He suffered from pains and headaches of such intensity that, after he had consulted a number of French doctors, his family sent him to a Swiss nursing home specializing in the treatment of nervous disorders. In 1920, after nearly two years in this establishment, Artaud's health seemed greatly improved and he expressed an ardent desire to go to Paris and write. The physician in charge, convinced that a return to the family in Marseilles could only prove detrimental to Artaud's health, suggested that his wish be granted. Since the family was agreeable to this plan, the doctor further recommended that Artaud be placed in the care of one Dr. Edouard Toulouse, chief of a clinic at Villejuif, a suburb of Paris. The choice was a happy one. The versatile psychiatrist was engaged in a literary effort as editor of a magazine called *Demain,* and to this modest periodical Artaud was soon to contribute articles and poems. Artaud's early poetic work reflects the influence of Poe and Baudelaire, both of whom he greatly admired. An atmosphere reminiscent of decadent and symbolist writings is suggested in these early poems, replete as they are with melancholia and world weariness. The real Artaud, who was far indeed from vague yearnings and gentle despondency, had not yet begun to express himself. Interviewed recently by Pierre Chaleix, Dr. Toulouse's widow recalled that her husband was immediately impressed by Artaud, certain that his gaunt and intense young patient belonged to the same race of men as Baudelaire, Gérard de Nerval, and Nietzsche. Madame Toulouse also recounts that her husband, in the belief that the greatest danger for men like Artaud lay in the extremes of intellectual inaction or too much work, took him on as a sort of collaborator, hoping that the tasks assigned to him would help Artraud maintain his equilibrium.[2] In this role, Artaud compiled an anthology of Toulouse's writings and prefaced it with an introduction.

Although Artaud had come to Paris because of his literary ambitions, once there, he found himself fascinated by the stage. His desire to act can be attributed both to his own deepest tendencies and to the fact that, although all the arts were in a state of considerable fermentation in the 1920's, nowhere was there more experimentation and excitement than in the theater. Here, a number of important directors were rebelling against naturalistic theatrical conventions which favored plays offering a "slice of life"—more often than not involving the most sordid aspects of contemporary life. Among these new directors was Lugné-Poe, who founded the Théâtre de l'Oeuvre in 1893. Interested in producing works of a symbolist and poetic nature, Lugné-Poe staged plays by Maeterlinck, Ibsen, Wilde, Alfred Jarry, Gide, and Claudel. A great admirer of Lugné-Poe, Artaud had the good fortune to begin his acting career under this avant-garde director. He obtained a small role in *Les scrupules de Sganarelle,* a play by the minor symbolist poet Henri de Régnier. Early in 1922, Firmin Gémier, an actor and director whose fame rests on his efforts to create a theater for the masses, saw and heard Artaud. Impressed by the young actor, Gémier recommended him to Charles Dullin, founder of the Théâtre de l'Atelier, one of the most important theatrical groups of that era. Dullin, who also rejected naturalism, laid great stress upon the mechanics of acting, such as breath and diction. Artaud's haunted face, his piercing intensity, so struck Dullin that he promptly accepted the young actor as a student and, later, as a member of his troupe. Under Dullin's direction Artaud played a number of roles, notably in Calderón's *La vida es sueño (Life Is a Dream)*, in Pirandello's *Il piacere dell'onestà (The Pleasure of Honesty)*, in Molière's *L'avare (The Miser)*, and in Cocteau's adaptation of Sophocles' *Antigone,* all of which were produced in 1922. Dullin recalls that Artaud was easy to work with, diligent and, when improvisation was required, gifted with a poet's imagination. Artaud obstinately refused, however, to have anything to do with the required mechanical exercises of diction. As is frequently the case, the student proved more radical than the teacher. Speaking of his own interest in the Oriental theater, Dullin remembers that Artaud "went much farther in this direction than I. From a practical viewpoint, that sometimes became dangerous; for example, in Pirandello's *The Pleasure of Honesty,* in which he played a businessman, he came on stage with make-up inspired by the little masks used by Chinese actors—a symbolic make-up which is slightly out of place in a modern comedy."[3] Another anecdote illuminating Artaud's relationship with Dullin is told by Jean-Louis Barrault. One day, during the rehearsal of a play in which Artaud was playing the role of the emperor Charlemagne, Artaud approached the throne on all fours. Thinking this interpretation too highly stylized, Dullin gently tried to persuade the actor that the role would be better played conventionally. At this, Artaud rose from the floor and replied with great disdain, "Oh! If you're concerned with truth! *Alors!*"[4]

Artaud's association with Dullin had important personal consequences for the young actor: through Dullin he met a fellow troupe member named Génica Athanasiou, a beautiful young woman of Greek extraction who was to enjoy a long acting career in Paris. She soon became Artaud's constant companion, and, although they broke apart in 1927, she is perhaps the only woman to have succeeded in sharing Artaud's life.

After Dullin, Artaud worked under Georges Pitoëff, another important actor–director of the 1920's. Pitoëff, greatly concerned with the idea of "modernism," produced the work of playwrights—Pirandello, for one—who reflected new trends of thought. During these years in the theater Artaud wandered from one Montparnasse hotel to another. Jean Hort remembers that when he met Artaud in 1923 (both were then working under Pitoëff at the Comédie des Champs-Elysées), Artaud frequently slept in the theater. Struck by the peculiar quality of Artaud's face and demeanor, his fellow actors agreed that he needed special roles—"angels or archangels, surrealistic demons, apocalyptic monsters, fantastic people." It was to Hort that Artaud confided his growing scorn for acting. On one occasion, when his friend expressed admiration for naturalistic, as opposed to expressionistic, acting, Artaud responded, "What's an actor? An instrument at rehearsals, a photograph to be reproduced, to redo what is already done."[5]

Even while occupied with the stage Artaud never ceased writing. Interested in art as well as literature, he published critical pieces on contemporary painters and writers. The first collection of his own poems appeared in 1923, under the title *Tric-trac du ciel (Backgammon of the Heavens)*. His poetic activities were carried on simultaneously with an examination of the nature of literary creation, and, indeed, of the process of thought itself. Artaud was tortured unceasingly by an inability to capture and express his thoughts. The ramifications of this problem constitute the major subject of a number of letters he wrote to Jacques Rivière, then editor of *la Nouvelle Revue Française*. Artaud and Rivière had begun a correspondence over some poems which Artaud had submitted to the magazine. Brushing aside the poems, Rivière urged Artaud to publish these letters. The result was the appearance, in 1927, of *Correspondance avec Jacques Rivière*. The attempt made by the young poet and the well-meaning editor to communicate was a sorry failure. Rivière, the experienced man of letters, could not grasp the nature or extent of Artaud's problems. Counseling the tortured young poet to exercise self-control and discipline, he assured Artaud that the problems facing him were those of all writers. Artaud insisted that he was absolutely alone and different from anyone else. Other poets, he asserted, "do not suffer and . . . I suffer, not only mentally, but physically, and in my everyday soul. This inability to relate to the object which characterizes all literature is, in my case, a failure to relate to life. As far as I'm concerned, I can truthfully say that I am not in the world, and that this is not simply an intellectual pose." (I, 39–40)

In the course of these early years in Paris Artaud met and was befriended by artists and writers who were already well known or about to become so—among them, Max Jacob, Michel Leiris, and André Masson. The latter, commenting in 1958 on Artaud's friendship with himself and the others, said that even Artaud's unconventional artist friends found him strange. "He was already different from us, he was particularly disturbed, there was something burning in him." Continuing his reminiscence, the painter goes on to say that Artaud's suffering "existed, but he played at it, he sought a plenitude of suffering. Artaud said to himself 'it is I who will play Artaud.' He didn't accept any relaxation . . . one day Aragon and I went dancing at the Zellis-Bar. Artaud was furious about it, he couldn't stand any amusements."[6]

In 1924 Artaud's father died, and his mother came to Paris to live with her son. (She was to remain with him until 1937.) It was during this same year that Artaud met and was immediately drawn to a number of Surrealists: André Breton, Robert Desnos, and Roger Vitrac. In these poets and artists Artaud recognized kindred spirits who, like himself, wanted to destroy traditional modes of European thought and culture in order to prepare the way for a rebirth of man's dormant inner life. André Breton, leader of the Surrealists, was so impressed by Artaud that he invited him to edit the third issue of the group's publication, *la Révolution surréaliste*. This issue contained a number of unsigned articles defining the beliefs and goals of the movement: *"Lettres aux recteurs des universités européennes"* ("Letters to the Chancellors of European Universities"), *"Adresse au Pape"* ("Address to the Pope"), *"Adresse au Dalaï-Lama"* ("Address to the Dalai Lama"), *"Lettres aux écoles de Bouddha"* ("Letters to the Followers of Buddha"), and *"Lettre aux médecins-chefs des asiles de fous"* ("Letter to the Medical Directors of Lunatic Asylums")—all bearing the stamp of Artaud's hand. Although Breton expressed reservations concerning these fiery letters at the time of their publication, years later he was to experience a radical change of heart: "I like these articles, especially those which best reflect Artaud's mark. I appreciate . . . the great role suffering played in leading him to this total rejection, which we all shared but which he formulated in the most fitting and ardent way."[7]

But Breton and the others could not really accept, much less encourage, Artaud's rejection of life and love. Artaud himself was soon to write that "what makes me different from the Surrealists is that they love life as much as I despise it." (I, 286) Nor could the other Surrealists identify themselves with the mystical aspirations expressed in a number of Artaud's poems. Breton complained that Artaud led him to a place which seemed "abstract, a gallery of ice . . . a place of lacunae and ellipses where personally I could no longer communicate with the innumerable things I like—things which, despite everything, keep me on this earth. It is too often forgotten that Surrealism loved many things and that it angrily condemned whatever was harmful to love."[8] At the same time, however, the Surrealist leader admitted that, in spite of Artaud's fundamental estrangement from the others, his contributions were important. "Perhaps he was in greater conflict than all of us with life. At that time, he was very handsome and whenever he moved, he called to mind the image of a Gothic nave pierced by lightning. He was possessed by a kind of fury which did not spare, so to speak, any human institutions . . . this fury, by its astonishing contagious power, profoundly influenced the course of Surrealism."[9]

Political differences were soon to deepen the existing temperamental cleavage between Artaud and other members of the Surrealist group. The acceptance of Marxist doctrines by some of the Surrealists horrified Artaud. No political doctrine, he asserted indignantly, could resolve the spiritual problems destroying man; politics could only distract men from confronting fundamental dilemmas. This immediate and instinctive reaction found warm support, years later, in the writings of Albert Camus. *The Rebel* sets forth Camus' conviction that an essential dichotomy irreparably separated the Surrealists, believers in the marvelous and in the forces of unreason, from the Marxists, whose basic doctrines were built on rationality and order. At the time, however, Artaud appears to have been the only one aware of all the implications of this fundamental dichotomy. Things came to a head in 1926 when Artaud (along with Philippe Soupault and Roger Vitrac) was "excommunicated" from the Surrealist group. Soon afterward, in 1927, he was violently attacked in a brochure entitled *"Au grand jour" ("In Broad Daylight"),* signed by Louis Aragon, André Breton, Paul Eluard, Benjamin Péret, and Pierre Unik, all of whom at the same time declared their allegiance to the Communist party. Intransigently condemning Artaud, they accused him of being concerned with the isolated pursuit of literature rather than with the welfare of man and society.

He [Artaud] only wanted to see a Revolution capable of metamorphosizing the soul's inner state. . . . He could not conceive of, nor did he recognize, anything other than what he called the "matter of his mind." Let us leave him to his detestable mixture of dreams, vague assertions, gratuitous insolences, to his manias. His hatreds—doubtless including his present hatred of Surrealism—are hatreds without dignity. He could never decide to strike unless he were sure that he could do so without danger or ill consequences. Among other things, it is amusing to note that this enemy of literature and art has always taken an active role only when his own literary interests were concerned, and that he has always chosen to deal with the most derisory objects, when nothing essential to life or mind was at stake.[10]

Artaud countered these accusations in a brochure of his own, *"A la grande nuit ou le bluff surréaliste" ("In the Dark of the Night: or, The Surrealist Bluff").* Declaring that political revolution alone was worthless because it could not effect a transformation of man's deepest nature, he berated the Surrealists for deriding him "when I speak of a metamorphosis of the soul's inner state, as if I imagined the soul in the same odious way that they do. Or, as if, from an absolute viewpoint, it could be of the slightest interest to see the social structure of the world changed, or to see power go from the hands of the bourgeoisie into those of the proletariat." (I, 284–285) Artaud categorically demanded something that would change man far more radically than could a simple political upheaval. Despite what was, to all appearances, a fairly bitter quarrel, in 1928 Breton saw fit to publish several new articles by Artaud in *la Révolution surréaliste*. But this was no more than the continuation of a purely professional relationship. It wasn't until 1936 that the friendship between the two men was resumed.

Despite his adventures, and misadventures, with the Surrealists, and his constant work in films and in the theater, Artaud found time to write two books in which his personal problems, as well as those involving literary creation and language, are minutely analyzed: *L'ombilic des limbes (The Umbilicus of Limbo)* and *Le pèse-nerfs (The Nerve-scale)*. Both volumes appeared in 1925. More poetic than his letters to Rivière, these books reveal Artaud's tormenting problems, particularly his inability to capture his thoughts and the ever-present sensation that his very being was escaping him. (*Le pèse-nerfs* was republished in 1927, followed by *"Fragments d'un journal d'enfer"* ["Fragments from a Diary of Hell"].)

Although his theatrical career had thus far been limited to acting, Artaud dreamed of establishing his own company to experiment with avant-garde plays and new methods of production. In 1926, in collaboration with Roger Vitrac (who had been "excommunicated" from the Surrealist group at the same time as Artaud) and Robert Aron, he founded such an experimental company with the financial support of Dr. René Allendy and the latter's wife. The company was named after Alfred Jarry, whose play *Ubu Roi* had shocked Paris in 1896. Artaud, who shared his contemporaries' enthusiasm for literary manifestoes, hailed the founding of the

Théâtre Alfred Jarry with a number of these documents. The first such manifesto demanded a theater capable of profoundly affecting its audience, and decreed that theatrical illusion "will no longer be concerned with the apparent truth or untruth of action, but with its communicative force and its reality. . . . We do not address ourselves to the mind or senses of the spectators, but to their whole existence." (II, 13) In the course of the ensuing three years, however, only eight performances were staged. The company, according to Artaud, was bedeviled by endless vicissitudes: the quest for capital, the choice of a theater, the difficulties inherent in collaboration, censorship, the police, competition, a derisive public, and intolerant critics. In spite of these problems Artaud was unshaken in his aims and maintained that the Théâtre Alfred Jarry would "contribute to the ruin of the theater as it currently exists in France, a ruin involving the destruction of all the literary or artistic ideas, all the psychological conventions, all the visual artifices, etc., upon which this theater is built." (II, 37)

Artaud's conception of drama was clearly anti-naturalistic; in fact, he sought a theater that would permit "all that is obscure, buried and unrevealed in the mind to manifest itself in a sort of real, material projection." (II, 22) He wanted the theater to unveil essential and universal truths through "impersonal" plays, written in collaboration so as to prevent individual particularities. Not until every individual viewpoint had been abandoned could a play be a "synthesis of all desires and all tortures." (II, 51) The original choice of plays clearly showed the company's intention to produce works which were not concerned with superficial, everyday reality but with man's most fundamental instincts. Artaud proposed that the company stage his own play *Le jet de sang (The Spurt of Blood)*, Alfred Jarry's *La peur chez l'amour* and *Le vieux de la montagne*, Roger Vitrac's *Les mystères de l'amour,* Robert Aron's *Gigogne,* Strindberg's *Le songe (A Dream Play),* and Cyril Tourneur's *The Revenger's Tragedy.* Not all these plays were produced but the Théâtre Alfred Jarry did present Artaud's *Le ventre brûlé ou la mère folle (Burnt Belly: or, The Crazy Mother),* Vitrac's *Les mystères de l'amour* and his *Victor ou les enfants au pouvoir,* Aron's *Gigogne,* the first act of Claudel's *Partage de midi,* and Strindberg's *Le songe.* During a performance of *Le songe,* on June 2, 1928, members of the Surrealist group staged a protest in the theater, provoking a disturbance which had to be quelled by the police. The Surrealists resented Artaud's preoccupation with the stage because they considered the theater decadent and bourgeois. They apparently failed to realize that Artaud shared their viewpoint and that all his efforts were directed to *changing* the conventional drama that they all abhorred. In addition, they claimed that Artaud had accepted aid from a politically corrupt government (Sweden) to produce this play. Breton's condemnation of Artaud was vehement, if somewhat less than rational. In his second "Manifesto of Surrealism," the spokesman for the Surrealists asserted that he

> would see nothing wrong if an actor, who wanted profits and notoriety, undertook to magnificently stage some play or other by Strindberg—a play which he himself did not consider important—if this same actor, from time to time, had not claimed to be a man of thought, anger and blood; if he were not the same man who burned, in certain pages of *la Révolution surréaliste,* if he can be believed, to burn everything . . . Alas! that was only a *role* for him like any other; he "staged" Strindberg's *Le songe* having learned that the Embassy of Sweden would pay. . . . I will always see M. Artaud at the door of the Alfred Jarry theater, flanked by two cops and pushing twenty others at the only people whom he had still acknowledged as friends the night before.[11]

Given Artaud's hatred for the "authorities" it scarcely seems possible that he would enlist the aid of the police. But such indeed was the case. In his discussion of the incident, Robert Aron recounts that the Surrealists had issued an "ultimatum" forbidding the Théâtre Alfred Jarry from giving a second performance of *Le songe*. Artaud and Aron informed Breton that they would not accede to this demand and turned to the police rather than surrender their freedom of action.

Despite the publicity resulting from this episode, the plight of the Théâtre Alfred Jarry grew steadily worse. In 1930 Artaud and Vitrac published a brochure, *"Le théâtre Alfred Jarry et l'hostilité publique,"* in which they summarized their accomplishments and appealed to the public for participation and support. Their plea went unheard and the entire venture collapsed. But the failure of this first experimental company did not destroy Artaud's ambition to succeed in the theater on his own terms. Shortly afterward he wrote to Louis Jouvet, one of the most important directors of that period, asking for a job as an assistant. Humbly, in sad contrast to his previous confident announcements concerning the Théâtre Alfred Jarry, Artaud assured Jouvet that

> I do not aspire to stage plays as a director. I can already see the derisive smile and the shrug that the mere thought of this must evoke in you. I need to eat; my inactivity weighs on me and it seems somewhat monstrous to be kept in the role of a mere actor. I will take the roles that are given to me; but, in addition, I am sure that if you are willing, and if you look for it, you will find a position in your theater that would suit me. (III, 203)

In a later letter, telling Jouvet of his need for important responsibilities as an antidote to instability, Artaud attributed the failure of the Théâtre Alfred Jarry to betrayal by "actors and circumstances." Artaud proved a persuasive correspondent; Jouvet took him on. Once employed, however, Artaud made no secret of his desire to stage plays himself. He complained to Jouvet repeatedly of inactivity and uselessness. Unfortunately, Jouvet, working in the more or less stylized French tradition, was not receptive to many of Artaud's more radical theories, and their collaboration was short-lived.

Given Artaud's great love for the theater, it was inevitable that he should find himself drawn to the nascent film industry. At first his enthusiasm for films was unreserved. "The cinema implies a total reversal of values, a complete transformation of optical viewpoints, of perspective, of logic. It is more exciting than phosphorus, more captivating than love." (III, 73) Only a few years later, however, his infatuation quelled by the introduction of talkies and the consequent commercialization of the industry, Artaud would denounce the cinema as "a frightful trade. Too many obstacles prevent you from expressing or realizing yourself. Too many commercial or financial contingencies constrain the directors I know. Too many men, things, and blind necessities are defended." (III, 110) He became increasingly convinced that talkies eliminated all the poetry and mystery of the screen. "The elucidation of words halts the unconscious and spontaneous poetry of images." (III, 98)

Artaud's cinematic career, which began with acting, spanned a long period of years. Even after his disillusionment with the medium, he continued to act since the money he earned in this way had become a vital source of income. His first roles, in Claude Autant-Lara's *Faits divers* (1922) and in René Clair's *Entr'acte* (1924), were modest ones. Soon, however, a number of important directors saw opportunities in Artaud's tortured appearance. Carl Dreyer, in his *La pas-*

sion de Jeanne d'Arc (1928), cast Artaud as a soulful monk torn between duty to his order and great love and compassion for Joan of Arc. Artaud's performance in this film has fascinated innumerable viewers, among them Anaïs Nin, who was moved to comment that Artaud "was beautiful . . . in the Carl Dreyer film. The deep-set eyes of the mystic, as if shining from caverns. Deep-set, shadowy, mysterious."[12] Abel Gance, too, understood the emotions that Artaud could convey, and cast him as the half-crazed Marat in his epic film *Napoléon* (1926) and as Savonarola in *Lucrèce Borgia* (1935). Artaud was apparently particularly well suited to play this last role; in a fictionalized account of a meeting with Artaud, Anaïs Nin compares him to the mad prophet:

> It was Savonarola looking at me, as he looked in Florence in the Middle Ages while his followers burned erotic books and paintings on an immense pyre of religious scorn. It was the same childish mouth of the monk, the deep-set eyes of the man living in the caverns of his separation from the world. Between us there was this holocaust burning, in his eyes the inquisitor's condemnation of all pleasure.[13]

Artaud felt a deep empathy with these tortured and half-crazed beings he portrayed. He knew, beyond any doubt, that he was the one to play the sinister Usher in Jean Epstein's version of *The Fall of the House of Usher*. "There is a quality of nervous suffering that the world's greatest actor cannot show in a film if he hasn't lived it. And I have lived it. I think like Usher." (III, 134–135)

Artaud's film career was not limited to acting. Just as he had wanted to establish a new theatrical company, so, too, did he desire to write and produce films. The second volume of the still-unfinished edition of his complete works contains a number of scenarios, many of which call to mind early Surrealistic films such as the Buñuel and Dali masterpiece *Un chien andalou* and Cocteau's *Le sang d'un poète (Blood of a Poet)*. In those scripts, objects metamorphose and disappear, normal time sequence is rearranged, and the line between dreams and reality is indiscernible. Only one of these scenarios was ever turned into a movie: in 1927 Germaine Dulac produced *La coquille et le clergyman (The Seashell and the Clergyman)*. Artaud had hoped to help direct it and to play the principal role of the clergyman, but Dulac delayed shooting for so long that Artaud, who had only a few weeks free for the project, was unable either to act in the film or to participate in its production.[14] Although *La coquille et le clergyman* has been highly praised and called the first true Surrealist film (antedating *Un chien andalou*), Artaud himself was bitterly disappointed with it. He accused Germaine Dulac of an artistic betrayal in filming certain scenes as dreamlike whereas for him they had been utterly real. She had thereby defeated his attempt to show that the illogic existed in the midst of what is normally considered reality. "This scenario is not the reproduction of a dream, and should not be regarded as such. I will not try to excuse its apparent incoherence by taking the simple escape route of dreams." (III, 23) Earlier, he had sought to produce plays revealing man's most basic instincts; now he hoped to create a film which would show the true workings of the mind. "*La coquille et le clergyman* does not tell a story; it develops a series of mental states which flow from one another, as thoughts flow from thoughts, without reproducing a rational chain of events." (III, 76) Conventional logic had to be banished from the film in order to reveal the underlying, profound reasons for our thoughts and emotions. Films, said Artaud, should allow us to perceive the occult and hidden aspects of life.

The first showing of *La coquille et le clergyman* took place on February 7, 1928, at the Studio des Ursulines.

Never one to keep silent when his own artistic aims were at stake, Artaud (and a selected group of friends) came to demonstrate at the film's première in protest against Dulac's "betrayal." This time it was Artaud himself who disrupted a presentation of his work. The February 18 issue of *Charivari* carried the following story of the occasion:

> The public followed with interest this curious production, until a voice in the room was heard asking this question: "Who made this film?"
> To which another voice answered, "Madame Germaine Dulac."
> First voice: "What is Madame Dulac?"
> Second voice: *"C'est une vache."*
> Hearing the vulgar term, Armand Tallier, the likable manager of the Studio, ran up, had the lights switched on and located the two troublemakers . . . It was Antonin Artaud, a slightly crazy and fanatical surrealist, the author of the scenario. In this way, he was demonstrating his displeasure with Mme. Dulac whom he accused of having distorted his "idea" (a slightly crazy idea).[15]

As a consequence of Mme. Dulac's production, Artaud became convinced that he must produce his scenarios himself. With the aid of René and Yvonne Allendy, he set out to establish a company to produce short films. This format, he believed, provided a fertile field for experimentation and would attract the same audience which had shown a ready appreciation of *Un chien andalou*. Convinced that a need for comic movies existed in France, Artaud also suggested that this company produce films like those of Mack Sennett in America. (In general, Artaud was a voluble enthusiast of early American films. He had great praise for the two Marx Brothers' films he saw—*Animal Crackers* and *Monkey Business*.) Artaud established his film company but no films were ever produced by it. However, a consequence of this abortive attempt was the close friendship that sprang up between Artaud and Dr. Allendy, one of the new venture's supporters. The two men shared a fascination for the occult sciences such as astrology and magic. Artaud's interest in esotericism was to grow increasingly stronger until, by 1937, he had become a full-fledged believer in the occult.

Through Allendy, Artaud met Anaïs Nin, who, at the time, was a great friend of Henry Miller. She won Artaud's admiration and, what was even more difficult, his confidence. Hers was a kindred spirit who could understand his tormenting problems. His letters to her, as well as her diary, bear eloquent witness to their brief but intense friendship. In one such letter, dated June 14, 1933, Artaud tells Miss Nin how touched he was by her reaction to a painting by Lucas van Leyden, and goes on to express his happiness over their friendship:

> You must understand the great unhappy joy, and even the stupefaction that I feel in having met you in this way. All at once I see my infinite emotional solitude filled, exactly, hermetically filled . . . destiny brings me more than everything I have dreamed of and wished for. . . . It would make me believe that miracles exist in this world, if I did not think that neither you nor I belong to this world.[16]

Anaïs Nin, for her part, was drawn to Artaud even while she resisted a romantic involvement. On one occasion Artaud asked her whether she feared that he was mad. She answered:

> I knew at that moment by his eyes, that he was, and that I loved his madness. I looked at his mouth, with the edges darkened by laudanum, a mouth I did not want to kiss. To be kissed by Artaud was to be drawn towards death, towards insanity; and I knew he wanted to be returned to life by

the love of woman, reincarnated, reborn, warmed, but that
the unreality of his life would make human love impossible.[17]

But her disinclination toward a romantic attachment with
Artaud did not lessen the great sympathy she felt for him.
"Such an immense pity I have for Artaud because he is always suffering. It is the darkness, the bitterness in Artaud I
want to heal. Physically I could not touch him, but the flame
and genius in him I love."[18]

Although Artaud managed to write feverishly during the
1920's, his ill-health was such that he grew to depend upon
drugs to alleviate the pain he suffered. (His need for drugs
was to remain constant throughout his life despite the peri-
odic attempts he made to rid himself of this unfortunate
habit.) Opium calmed his nervous disorders, and served, at
the same time, to stimulate his poetic imagination. Like
Coleridge and Baudelaire before him, Artaud put to literary
use the hallucinations experienced under drugs. A number
of prose poems, describing these hallucinatory visions, were
published in 1929 under the title *L'art et la mort (Art and
Death)*. The publisher of this volume, Robert Denoël, sub-
sequently suggested to Artaud that he undertake a translation of Matthew Gregory Lewis' *The Monk,* a Gothic tale
replete with numerous passages of sex and sadism. The result, Artaud's *Le moine,* was published in 1931 and proved
to be more an adaptation of the Lewis work than a translation. Part of Artaud's attraction to *The Monk* undoubtedly
stemmed from his affiliation with the Surrealists, who admired Gothic novels in which rationality and logic are
pushed aside as the world of reason is transcended by that of
imagination. (Breton, for example, praised *The Monk* for its
"marvelous" elements: "In the literary domain, only the
marvelous is capable of rendering fruitful works that belong
to an inferior genre such as the novel. . . . *Le moine* attests

to this admirably. The breath of the marvelous animates it completely."[19]) Artaud himself stated that he was drawn to the book through his interest in supernatural and occult phenomena; Lewis' matter-of-fact treatment of supernatural occurrences greatly appealed to him. *"The Monk,* for me, was valuable because the natural was introduced into supernatural workings, while the Marvelous became a manageable object, a state into which you could enter as you enter another room by opening the door and pushing aside the curtain." (IV, 403)

Following the publication of *Le moine,* Bernard Steele, Denoël's associate in publishing, collaborated with Artaud on a translation of a book by Ludwig Lewisohn, *Crime passionnel.* These two books appear to have stimulated Artaud's taste for blood and gore. Shortly after the latter volume appeared, he began work on a study of the Roman emperor Heliogabalus—a tyrant whose fame rests on tales of extreme cruelty and flamboyant homosexuality, as well as on the sexual perversions for which his reign was notorious. To document his book, Artaud plunged into an extensive examination of the ancient Middle Eastern religions and solar cults associated with Heliogabalus' epoch. The result was *Héliogabale ou l'anarchiste couronné (Heliogabalus: or, The Crowned Anarchist),* published in 1934. In reply to a letter from Jean Paulan inquiring about the historical accuracy of *Héliogabale,* Artaud answered that it did not matter whether his book was true or not. If it conveyed the idea of a "Superior Reality," that would transcend mere facts. Historical data only served as a starting point. "I wanted the Esoteric Truths to be true in spirit; their form is often FALSE deliberately. But form is nothing. There are excesses and exaggerations of images, wild affirmations; an atmosphere of panic is established in which the rational loses ground while the spirit advances in arms." (VII, 185)

Le moine, Crime passionnel, and *Héliogabale* reveal Artaud's interest in the occult as well as in sexuality and violence. This fascination with the darker, more mysterious aspects of human existence was to play an increasingly important role in Artaud's slowly developing concept of the theater. The stage, to which Artaud constantly returned, was his major passion and remained so until his death. His last work, a radio broadcast entitled *Pour en finir avec le jugement de dieu (To end god's judgment),* was to have been the final triumph of his Théâtre de la Cruauté. Artaud's fascination with the theater inspired his book *Le théâtre et son double (The Theater and Its Double),* which was published in 1938. Considered by many to be Artaud's magnum opus, this book has grown in influence to the point where it is today virtually impossible to discuss contemporary theater and theatrical experiments, such as Happenings or the Living Theater, without mentioning Artaud. *Le théâtre et son double* is a compilation of lectures and articles written in the early 1930's. The most powerful essay is probably *"Le théâtre et la peste,"* in which Artaud, drawing a parallel between the plague and theatrical action, maintains that dramatic activity must be able to effect a catharsis in the spectator even as the plague purifies mankind. Prior to its publication, the article was the basis of a lecture at the Sorbonne. Anaïs Nin, who, along with Allendy, was in the audience, recalls that Artaud started the lecture in a normal voice. Then:

> . . . imperceptibly almost, he let go of the thread we were following and began to act out dying by plague. . . .
>
> His face was contorted with anguish, one could see the perspiration dampening his hair. His eyes dilated, his muscles became cramped, his fingers struggled to retain their flexibility. He made one feel the parched and burning throat, the pains, the fever, the fire in the guts. He was in

agony. He was screaming. He was delirious. He was enacting
his own death, his own crucifixion.

At first people gasped. And then they began to laugh.
Everyone was laughing! They hissed. Then one by one, they
began to leave, noisily, talking, protesting. They banged the
door as they left.[20]

Seated in a café after the lecture, Artaud confided to Anaïs
Nin that he had deliberately let himself go in an attempt to
make his audience experience the plague itself, "so that they
will be terrified and awaken. I want to awaken them. They
do not realize *they are dead*." That may have been Artaud's
motive, but, as Miss Nin remarks, the audience was incapable of understanding, or even tolerating, him: "What a shock
to see a sensitive poet confronting a hostile public. What
brutality, what ugliness in the public!"[21]

In *"Sur le théâtre balinais,"* another important essay in
Le théâtre et son double, Artaud expresses his admiration of
an Oriental theatrical group which had come to Paris. Longing for a theater with a metaphysical orientation like that of
ancient Greece or the Orient, Artaud rejects Western theater
for its traditional preoccupation with psychological and social problems. His ideal theater would resemble the Oriental
stage in which gestures often replace spoken language. Further, all the non-verbal elements of theater—sounds, lighting, music, decor—would assume roles of prime importance.

Undaunted by the failure of his Théâtre Alfred Jarry,
Artaud continued his efforts to establish a theater company
that would realize his dramatic concepts. Not surprisingly,
this hope was expressed in still another literary manifesto
entitled *"Le théâtre de la cruauté."* This essay, first published in *la Nouvelle Revue Française,* was later included in
Le théâtre et son double. It describes the technique, the
themes, and the proposed program of the company envisaged
by its author. The term "theater of cruelty," by which Ar-

taud designated a theater capable of awakening man to the cruelty inherent in life, has since become an accepted part of the vocabulary of the theater. In 1933, with the encouragement and help of his publishers, Robert Denoël and Bernard Steele, Artaud managed to establish an actual company called *Le théâtre de la Cruauté*. To raise the necessary financial support, Artaud gave a reading of *Richard II* on January 6, 1934, at the home of a novelist friend, Madame Lise Deharme.

Despite Artaud's feverish enthusiasm, he failed both in raising sufficient money and in arousing public interest in his venture; the Théâtre de la Cruauté proved no more successful than the Théâtre Alfred Jarry. Only one play, *Les Cenci*, was produced. Written by Artaud himself, *Les Cenci* was adapted from the story of the Cenci family found in Stendhal's *Chroniques italiennes* and in Shelley's play *The Cenci*. Like so many of the books Artaud was writing and adapting during these years, the play, produced on May 6, 1935, abounds with scenes of sex and sadism. Artaud himself played the role of Cenci, an Italian nobleman obsessed by an incestuous desire for his daughter whom he eventually tortures and kills. Up to this point in his career, Artaud's dramatic works had been few: in addition to *Le ventre brûlé ou la mère folle*, he had written a short surrealistic play called *Le jet de sang* (included in *L'ombilic des limbes*), a pantomime with words entitled *La pierre philosophale* (*The Philosopher's Stone*), and an adaptation (since lost) of Seneca's bloody tragedy *Atreus and Thyestes*. *Les Cenci*, intended to dispense with the psychological problems of individuals, was to reveal the forces of destiny at work and, at the same time, to embody many of Artaud's theories on staging and dramatic effects. But even Artaud's admirers found it difficult to praise the play which, at several points, disintegrates into pure melodrama. The critical reviews were harsh, with the notable exception of Pierre Jean Jouve, who believed that *Les Cenci* had greatly affected its audience. "This theater is not made to please. Artaud constantly plays against the house and wins. The spectator is continually upset, and sometimes hurt, by the sharpest tension."[22] The adverse critical reception of the play did nothing to alleviate the financial difficulties, and the company met the same fate as had Artaud's earlier Théâtre Alfred Jarry. With the company's dissolution ended Artaud's last major theatrical venture.

The failure of the Théâtre de la Cruauté engendered a bitterness and disappointment so acute as to lead to a decision to abandon all theatrical activity. Attributing his lack of success to European decadence and sterility, Artaud began to dream of a land uncontaminated by Western culture, a land where ancient beliefs and pagan customs continued to exert a powerful influence. As it attracted D. H. Lawrence, Henri Michaux, and others, so now did Mexico beckon to Artaud. It was there that he hoped to find a civilization where the cosmic forces that he had attempted to present on stage still existed, and in their purest form.

> I have come to Mexico to make contact with the Red Earth
> and it stinks just like it smells sweet
> it smells good just like it was stinking
>
> (CG)

Never one to dream idly, Artaud set out for Mexico on January 10, 1936. Having long since become a devotee of magic and the occult, it is not surprising that he should have attributed great importance to the two "magical" items that he brought with him to Mexico, carefully guarding them on the journey. One was a cane—given him by René Thomas—that was said to have belonged to a magician from Savoy. Artaud was convinced that St. Patrick had spoken of this cane, and that Christ Himself had used it in His struggle with the demons. The other object was a small sword that a Negro magician had given Artaud, as a souvenir, when the ship put in at Havana.

Once in Mexico, Artaud was plagued by financial difficulties and he was forced to write to his friends in Paris, among them Jean-Louis Barrault, for help. He had left France with very little money, determined, as he said, to risk everything to effect a radical change in his life. To cover the cost of modest living expenses, he gave a few lectures at the University of Mexico and wrote some articles. Many of the French texts of these lectures and articles have been lost, with the result that they can now be found only in Spanish, in a book entitled *México,* published by the University of Mexico in 1962.

Artaud was not content to remain in cosmopolitan Mexico City, for he had come to this land to find a primitive and uncontaminated culture. With the aid of the University of Mexico he embarked on a mission to the interior of Mexico to study the ancient Indian races in order to "find and revive any vestiges of the ancient Solar culture." Filled with enthusiasm for this venture, Artaud confided to René Thomas, on April 2, 1936, "I am leaving to seek the impossible. All the same, we shall see if I am going to find it. When you learn what it's all about and that they listened to me seriously in official circles when I declared what I wanted to do, you will believe that there are Gods and that they are on my side." (T, 149)

In the mountains of northern Mexico, Artaud sought out the Tarahumara tribe, famous for its rituals involving the use of peyote, an hallucinogenic drug. Artaud became an eager participant in these rites which went on, uninterruptedly, for days. His poetic account of this stay with the Indians constitutes the major portion of his book *D'un voyage au pays des Tarahumaras (Concerning a Journey to the*

Land of the Tarahumaras) which did not appear until 1945. Artaud's excitement over the Tarahumara civilization is evident in a letter he wrote to Jean Paulhan: "What I see in Mexico shows me that I have always been on the right road. . . . It is necessary for Gallimard to know that the Revolution is fermenting *everywhere* and that it is a Revolution *for* culture, *in* culture . . . and that madness, utopia, the unreal and the absurd will constitute reality." (V, 277–278)

Whatever the attractions, Artaud did not wish to remain in Mexico indefinitely and November 1936 found him back in Europe. In an attempt to readjust to something approximating a normal life, he submitted to cures for drug addiction and even became engaged to Cécile Schramme, a youthful middle-class Belgian. Conceivably, he thought that she could halt his increasing estrangement from the world, for at times he would write to her as if she were an angel sent to redeem and help him. Other letters, however, bespeak his growing obsession with purity and sex. At such times he reproaches her violently for her sexuality. "I have confidence in your idea of absolute love, and in your will to attain it, not in your behavior *which is weak and bestial*." (VII, 211) The engagement miraculously survived until Artaud came to Brussels in May 1937 to give a lecture on his Mexican adventures. Two versions of what happened on that occasion have since circulated. According to one, Artaud appeared in front of the audience and announced, "Since I've lost my notes, I am going to speak about the effect of masturbation on the Jesuit fathers." According to the other version, seemingly more trustworthy, Artaud began his address uneventfully before a staid audience, but his tone grew increasingly more violent as the lecture proceeded. Finally, his face contorted in agony, he screamed insanely, "In revealing all that to you, I may have killed myself." (VII, 439)

This incident marked the beginning of many dark years for Artaud. In the next few months he moved further and further from the world of ordinary men. His alienation may have been heightened by a number of factors: the hallucinogenic drugs he had used in Mexico, shock upon finding himself back in Europe relatively unknown and unsuccessful, and, most likely of all, an intensification of the nervous disorders which had plagued him all his life. It is difficult to say whether his feelings of estrangement led him to plunge deeper and deeper into the magical arts, or whether his interest in the occult drew him further and further away from the everyday world. Whatever the case, Artaud's obsession with the occult became complete. Manuel Cano de Castro, who, in the spring of 1937, had taught Artaud how to play the tarot cards, remembers that as soon as Artaud had the cards in his hands nothing else mattered. He became utterly immersed in them and, according to de Castro, showed "a perfect mastery of the analogical interpretation of symbols and numbers . . . , of this vast synthesis of magical cards, using them with ease, as if he possessed great practice, led by his astonishing divinatory sense." Artaud read in the cards that the world would be destroyed. And, says de Castro, as soon as Artaud understood the terrifying message of the cards, "the frightening vision of what was to happen to the world haunted him. He could no longer rest."[23]

Another consequence of Artaud's immersion in the occult was a conviction that his name had to disappear. His article *"D'un voyage au pays des Tarahumaras"* was published in *la Nouvelle Revue Française* of August 1937 with the name of the author replaced by three stars. To Jean Paulhan he wrote, "In a short while I will be dead or in a situation such that I will not need a name. I am therefore counting on you for the 3 Stars." (VII, 227) He began to sign many of his letters with the symbol Δ ♀ Δ. To Manuel Cano de Castro he confided that the cards had told him that a woman would come who would deliver him from all that menaced him, a woman marked "by the astonishing virtue of asceticism."

Artaud's belief that the future had been revealed to him by the tarot cards gradually led to his conviction that supernatural truths had been communicated to him and that it was his mission to reveal them to mankind. In a letter to Anne Manson, a young journalist he had met in Paris, he describes his new vocation: "My Path is the True Path, and he who does not serve my Path is Himself off any Path! ! To be with me means to leave all the rest. Whoever is unable to leave all the rest cannot be with me." (VII, 247) Like a prophet of the Old Testament, Artaud announces worldwide doom in his short book *Les nouvelles révélations de l'être (The New Revelations of Being)*, published in 1937 and signed "Le Révélé." Predicting a coming apocalypse, he declares his complete alienation from the rest of mankind. "It is a truly Desperate Man who is speaking to you and who knows the happiness of being in the world only now that he has left it and is absolutely separated from it." (VII, 151)

Increasingly estranged from the world, in the summer of 1937 Artaud set about making arrangements for a trip to Ireland. He arrived in Cóbh on August 14, 1937. Suffering from the delusion that his cane was the former property of St. Patrick, it seemed only proper that he return it to its place of origin. Apart from the cane, Ireland fascinated him because of its aura of magic and legend; just as he had wanted to find a primitive culture in Mexico, so, too, did he hope to find traces of the ancient druids in Ireland. But the journey only served to aggravate his nervous condition, for his letters from Ireland reflect ever-increasing aberrations. With a sense of great urgency he sent warnings to his friends in Paris that the world would soon be destroyed by an earth-shattering cataclysm, and that a tragic cycle of human history was drawing to a close. (Curiously enough, the date Artaud predicted for this coming apocalypse was 1940.) Strangely blending occult and mystical doctrines, he sought to understand the religious and spiritual principles controlling the universe. To Anne Manson he wrote, "Pushed by gigantic forces I finally discovered who I was and to accept what I was. The Voice of christ reveals to me every day the doctrine of life and death, the mystery of birth and Incarnation. I know, *alas,* I know how the world was made and I have received the *Mission* to reveal it to the whole world." (VII, 278). Fascinated by the analogies existing among all religious systems, he dwelt upon the idea that God had come to earth in different incarnations, such as Christ and the Hindu Krishna. Believing that he himself had been sent to earth by a purposeful God, he saw himself as mankind's new spiritual savior, sent by Jesus to do battle with the Antichrist. His cane, which came from Christ Himself, would help him in his fight. "I must reveal to you, Anne," he wrote, "that in a few days (about 30) I will speak publicly In the Name of God Himself." (VII, 281)

Artaud went from Cóbh to Galway then to Kiltona, and, finally, to Dublin. Judging by his violent and aggressive letters, it would appear that his mental state grew steadily worse. In a letter to Anne Manson dated September 15, 1937, he commanded her to tell his erstwhile friends in Paris that "I will not return alone, but with an army. If they believe I am crazy, suffering from megalomania, or raving, so much the worse for them. . . .Tell them that I have hated them for years, them and their political, social, moral, amoral and immoral ideas." (VII, 294)

It was in Dublin that Artaud became a convert to Catholicism. Five years later he explained to Jean-Louis Barrault that "Antonin Artaud returned to the Church and the Catholic and Christian faith of the Church of Jesus Christ,

in Dublin, in September 1937, and he confessed and took
Communion one Sunday morning in a church in this town
where he had come to bring back St. Patrick's cane which
you had seen in his hand in Paris, in June, July and August
of 1937."[24] Following his conversion, Artaud repudiated almost all his earlier writings as atheistic and blasphemous, ex-
cepting, however, his *Correspondance avec Rivière, Le
théâtre et son double,* and *Les nouvelles révélations de
l'être.*

In Dublin without funds and in a highly agitated state
of mind, he sought refuge at a Jesuit college. At the college
entrance his knocking met with no response and he began
to scream and hammer at the door. The police were soon
called and as a result of the ensuing fight St. Patrick's cane
disappeared and Artaud was imprisoned for six days. The
police searched his clothes and finding nothing of an in-
criminating nature released him on condition that he
promptly return to France. Meanwhile his friends in Paris,
receiving no word from Artaud, began to worry. When Jean
Paulhan made inquiries concerning Artaud's whereabouts,
the French consul replied:

> The Irish police made M. Artaud's presence in Dublin
> known to the French legation at the end of last September
> (1937). They expressed the desire of sending our compatriot,
> who was without resources and in a state of high exaltation,
> back to France. The legation intervened as much as possi
> ble in favor of M. Artaud who embarked at Cóbh on Septem-
> ber 29, on the *Washington,* and must have arrived the fol-
> lowing morning at Le Havre.[25]

During the course of the return voyage aboard the *Washing-
ton,* an episode occurred which was to seal Artaud's fate for
the next nine years. While seated on his bunk, two members
of the crew, a steward and a mechanic, brusquely entered

his room. Artaud, feeling himself persecuted and threatened, greeted them with a menacing gesture. The fight which followed ended in Artaud's arrest. When the ship arrived at Le Havre there was no one to protect or defend Artaud. The authorities, aware of what had happened in Ireland, had him certified as mad and placed him in a mental institution. This was the first of a series of institutions which were to include Sotteville-les-Rouen, Sainte-Anne, Ville-Evrard, and, finally, Rodez.

During the early years of his confinement, Artaud was completely withdrawn, refusing to see friends or to write to them. His first letters, sent from Ville-Evrard, where he stayed from February 1939 to January 1943, describe the humiliations he endured in the ward for drug addicts to which, head shaven and in the uniform of the inmates, he had been assigned. He appealed pathetically to his friends for help. To Roger Blin (a well-known contemporary director whose productions reveal the influence of Artaud), he begged: "If you have some true affection for me—as I felt you did the other day—make an additional effort for me and don't tell me: I am going to try and if I have the opportunity I will do it. Say to yourself: I am going to do that because he is suffering; it is absolutely urgent and necessary."[26] But France was occupied by Hitler's armies and neither Artaud's friends nor his mother could really help him. Finally his faithful poet friend Robert Desnos succeeded in convincing Dr. Gaston Ferdière, director of the asylum at Rodez, to rescue Artaud from the hellish conditions he endured at Ville-Evrard where he had made virtually no progress. In fact, when Robert Desnos saw Artaud at Ville-Evrard he was appalled by what had happened to his friend. As he wrote to Ferdière, he had found Artaud delirious and speaking as if he were St. Jerome. "[He was] no longer eager to leave because he was being parted from the magic forces working for him. . . . It had been five years since I had seen him and his exaltation and his madness were a painful sight for me. I persuaded his mother to pay no attention to his speeches and to allow him to leave insofar as I am sure that he would be better off with you."[27] Finally, on February 11, 1943, Artaud was transfered to the more enlightened institution of Rodez.

The treatment Artaud received at Rodez has been the source of bitter disputes and enmity. His friends, who maintain that Artaud was not mad and did not need to be committed at all, become enraged simply at the mention of Ferdière's name. Well-meaning undoubtedly, Dr. Ferdière decided upon a course of treatment that rested heavily on electric shock treatments of which Artaud complained with great anguish: "I died at Rodez under electric shock. I say dead. Legally and medically dead."[28] Ferdière, on the other hand, staunchly maintains that Artaud was indeed mad and required such treatments. Although the poet might have appeared quite reasonable, he was dangerously anti-social and suffered from deliriums which rendered him "dangerous to public order and the security of people." As further proof of Artaud's madness, Ferdière reminds us that Artaud dedicated *Les nouvelles révélations de l'être* to Adolf Hitler, and moreover, that his religious convictions changed daily. The chaplain at Rodez never knew whether he would find Artaud in the midst of prayer or in a violently abusive mood. Ferdière also recounts that when he and his wife invited Artaud to dinner, the poet displayed disgusting eating habits and went down on his knees to pray in the middle of the meal. Only when the doctor handed him his little sword did Artaud seem reassured.[29] Even if Artaud was not completely cured at Rodez, argues Ferdière, the treatment he received there enabled him to begin anew his life as a creative artist. However laudable Ferdière's intentions may have been,

Artaud resented the man of science no less than his own abject helplessness. Deeply bitter over his treatment at Rodez, in many of his later poems Artaud violently castigates doctors, and numerous passages in his book on Van Gogh are devoted to a condemnation of psychiatry. "It is foully impossible to be a psychiatrist without being marked, at the same time, by the stamp of the most indisputable insanity: the insanity of not being able to fight against this atavistic reflex of the black earth which makes every scientist caught in the black earth a kind of born innate enemy of all geniuses." (VG, 32) Nor does Artaud stop at accusing Van Gogh's physician, Dr. Gachet, of having killed his patient.

Whatever one may say or think of the treatment he received at Dr. Ferdière's clinic, it is undeniable that it was at Rodez that Artaud, who had been silent for so many years, began to write again. And not only to write, but to paint and draw. Under Ferdière's care, Artaud composed his haunting *Lettres de Rodez (Letters from Rodez)* in which he describes, with perfect clarity, abnormal states of mind. In fact, all of Artaud's writing of this period reveals a curious mixture of lucidity and aberration. In one of his letters from Rodez, for example, he explains coherently and convincingly that he is being bewitched and crucified by demons, and that his "internment is the result of a shocking occult plot in which all sects of initiated christians, catholics, jews, buddhists and brahmans . . . have participated." (R, 38) His obsessions revolved around sex, bodily functions, magic, and religion. A letter dated July 19, 1943, written to one of his doctors, Jacques Latrémolière, is illustrative. "As for me, I consider sex to be an infamy and I will not allow a man who is not chaste to come and reproach me with seeing and sensing demons. The fact that he does not remain strictly virginal means that he must assume his share of human responsibility for the production of evil spirits."[30]

His horror of sexuality is at least partially responsible for his violent outbursts of Catholicism, for he was sure that this religion confirmed his hatred of sex and his reverence for purity. His mystical, quasi-Catholic feelings, combined with his former belief that he was a prophet, led to the conviction that he had been entrusted with the divine mission of restoring man to his original state of purity and chastity. "A man had been commissioned by God to recall all these truths on earth; this man was named Antonin Artaud, and he fought in Paris for years to affirm this celestial mission. You cannot say that this is not true for there are innumerable witnesses of these battles which have left their mark in books and newspapers."[31] At times, he was convinced that he was Christ, and that Jesus had stolen his identity from him. Incredible as it may appear, sincere Catholics (François Mauriac among them) see in Artaud's fleeting aberrations a true conversion to Catholicism.[32] Toward the end of his stay in Rodez, Artaud repudiated his conversion and began a violent attack on the Church. To Henri Parisot he stated that "the christ is always what I have most abominated," and in Les Tarahumaras he insisted that his conversion was the result of a terrible spell that had been cast upon him.

With the end of World War II, Artaud was visited at Rodez by a number of his friends—Jean Dubuffet, Marthe Robert, Arthur Adamov, Colette and Henri Thomas, and André Berne-Joffroy. Led by Arthur Adamov and Marthe Robert, they organized a committee to effect Artaud's release from the asylum. Dr. Ferdière, who favored the committee's efforts, agreed to discharge Artaud in the custody of his friends (rather than his family, as was the usual procedure) provided financial guarantees were made to ensure that his patient would not be destitute. To satisfy the practical-minded doctor, a benefit performance was organized by Jean Paulhan. On June 17, 1946, a number of celebrated actors read Artaud's poems at the Sarah Bernhardt Theater, and ten days later a sale was organized of manuscripts and paintings which included contributions from Dubuffet and Picasso.

Finally, on May 26, 1946, after nine years, Artaud left Rodez—his health completely ruined. His face was ravaged and white, his cheeks sunken. All his teeth had been lost as a result of the shock treatments. He was painfully thin. Whether or not he should have been released from Rodez, whether his mental and physical condition required further treatment, are questions which have since been bitterly debated. His sister, Marie-Ange Malausséna, insists that his friends did Artaud a great disservice:

> But in 1946 came the intervention of people who, with an impudent, indifferent attitude toward the poet's mother, decided, without informing her, to obtain Antonin Artaud's liberty from Dr. Ferdière under the pretext of taking charge of him.
>
> They obtained this liberty. From then on, the poet was lost.
>
> Free to roam around Paris, he managed to procure drugs with a chloral base and vials of laudanum.[33]

To this last charge Artaud's friends have replied that the poet was forced to take drugs to combat the pain of a cancer which had surprisingly not been diagnosed at Rodez. It is difficult to ascertain whether or not Artaud's mental state was "cured" upon release from the institution. Fredière himself believes that Artaud's condition was incurable, that medicine had done all that was possible. Asked about Artaud's "madness" upon leaving Rodez, André Breton answered that the poet was relatively stable except when certain sensitive topics came up. His friends made every possible effort to avoid such topics, but this was not always possible. For instance, recounts Breton, Artaud believed that when he disembarked at Le Havre, a riot had been contrived to prevent certain revelations that he wanted to make and that, in the ensuing violence, Breton had been killed trying to help Artaud. One day at the Café des Deux-Magots, Breton told Artaud that he could not recall the incident. Artaud became very upset and insisted that Breton was being deceived by occult powers.[34]

Upon his discharge from Rodez, Artaud was ostensibly free to go where he pleased. It was apparent, however, that he was in need of constant care. His friends, accordingly, arranged for him to stay at the nursing home of Dr. Achille Delmas at Ivry, on the outskirts of Paris. At Ivry he asked for and obtained a private lodge. By a strange coincidence, the one assigned to him had reputedly housed Gérard de Nerval, whom Artaud considered a spiritual ancestor. During the two years that followed, Artaud never ceased writing poems. Many of them were dictated to Paule Thévenin, the woman who had arranged for him to stay at Ivry and who was to be his constant and devoted companion for the rest of his life. She is now perhaps the only one alive able to decipher many of the manuscripts. Although in ill-health, Artaud still required the stimulation that Paris offered, and he was frequently seen in his old Left Bank haunts. But merely to be in Paris and to see his old friends was not enough; he wanted to play an important role in the intellectual and literary life of Paris, as he had in the 1920's. Toward this end, he consented to give a lecture at the Vieux Colombier Theater entitled *"Tête-à-tête, par Antonin Artaud,"* in which he intended to tell the story of his life. On the night of January 13, 1947, he addressed an audience

which included André Gide, Jean-Louis Barrault, Jean Vilar,
André Breton, Roger Blin, Jean Paulhan, Arthur Adamov,
Henri Pichette, and Albert Camus. With hindsight it is
clear that his old associates should have prevented this performance. In the course of the lecture, Artaud was suddenly
seized with panic and scattered his papers all over the floor.
He made a feeble effort to continue by improvising, but
then, terror-stricken, he fled from the room. His fear and
anguish had evidently communicated themselves to the audience, for Maurice Saillet later reported:

> When he came on stage, with his thin and ravaged face,
> looking like Edgar Allan Poe and Baudelaire at the same
> time; when his passionate hands fluttered like birds and
> groped untiringly around his face; when his hoarse voice,
> broken by sobs and tragic stammers, began to deliver his
> beautiful, but scarcely audible poems, we felt ourselves swept
> up into a dangerous zone, as if we were sucked in by this
> black sun, caught up by this "spreading combustion" of a
> body which was prey to the flames of the spirit.[35]

Artaud was so touched by Saillet's comments that he wrote
the latter telling him of his inability to express himself in
words, and of his conviction that the world was nothing but
a place where "all the rare lucid tortured souls have always
been assassinated."[36] But perhaps the most eloquent witness
of this unfortunate lecture was André Gide, who was moved
to write:

> Leaving this memorable séance, the public grew silent.
> What was there to say. They had just seen a pitiful man,
> atrociously shaken by a god, as if on the sill of a deep grotto,
> the sibyl's secret cave where nothing profane is tolerated,
> where, as on a poetic Carmel, a prophet, simultaneously
> priest and victim, is exposed and offered to thunderbolts and
> devouring vultures . . . One felt ashamed to assume one's
> place in a world where comfort is made of compromises.[37]

Shortly after the lecture at the Vieux Colombier, Artaud attended an exhibit of Van Gogh's paintings which deeply impressed him. A few days later, upon reading an article by a psychiatrist who declared that Van Gogh was mad, Artaud became so indignant that he promptly began to write a book on the Dutch painter. It has already been mentioned that Artaud used this book to castigate doctors and psychiatrists, and, indeed, all of society. "It is thus that society has strangled in her asylums everybody she wanted to get rid of . . . because they refused to make themselves her accomplices in certain important filthy affairs." (VG, 14) Considered by many Artaud enthusiasts to be the poet's most beautiful work, written poetically and simply, *Van Gogh, le suicidé de la société (Van Gogh: The Man Suicided by Society)* enjoyed a great success and, in 1947, won the coveted Sainte-Beuve literary prize. This same year saw the publication of two of Artaud's most important poems: *Artaud le Momo* and *Ci-gît, précédé de la culture indienne (Here lies, preceded by Indian culture)*. The fact that both poems center around the body and its attendant ills is not surprising, for at this time the cancer which had attacked Artaud was growing increasingly more painful. Opium no longer sufficed to quell the pain, and he had taken to doses of chloral which provoked quasi comas and debilitated him still further.

Despite his illness, Artaud never stopped working. In July 1947, the Galerie Pierre was the scene of another exhibition of his drawings. On this occasion he read a number of recently written poems. Soon afterward, Fernand Pouey, then working for the French Broadcasting Company (Radio-diffusion Française), asked Artaud if he would write a radio script to be broadcast February 2, 1948. To Artaud, who continued to cherish his hopes for a new theater, a "theater of cruelty" capable of electrifying its audience, this was a welcome opportunity. In relatively quick order he finished the poem

Pour en finir avec le jugement de dieu, which was intended as the script for the broadcast. Following its completion, Artaud came to Paris from Ivry every day to attend rehearsals and to supervise the sound effects which were to play an important role. The poetic script was to be read by Artaud himself, the faithful Paule Thévenin, Roger Blin, and the noted actress, Maria Casarès. But the evening before the scheduled broadcast, the director of the Broadcasting Company, Wladimir Porché, decided to cancel the event for fear of the public's reaction to certain passages. (The script, like most of Artaud's later works, is replete with words generally considered obscene.) Pouey, however, disagreed with Porché, and invited some fifty important people to listen to a private studio broadcast of the poem. Among those present were Jean-Louis Barrault, Raymond Queneau, Roger Vitrac, Louis Jouvet, and Paul Eluard. Despite the enthusiastic reception they gave to Artaud's work, Porché did not relent and the ban was maintained. This gave rise to a heated campaign in the press. In a letter to Porché, Artaud, who was hurt and bitterly disappointed by the entire episode, admits that there are violent words in his poem, but he insists that they occur in an "atmosphere so removed from life that I do not think that any public exists which could be scandalized by them." (JD, 91)

In a letter to Bettina Knapp, Paule Thévenin narrates movingly the events of Artaud's last days.[38] It was during the period of his daily visits to Paris from Ivry, early in 1948, that the deterioration in Artaud's health became a matter of serious concern to his good friend Paule and her physician husband. Emaciated, complaining constantly of intestinal pains, the poet was consuming alarming quantities of chloral and of laudanum. To the suggestion of the Thévenins that he consult a specialist, Artaud replied that nine years in asylums would ruin anyone's digestive system. When the pain became intolerable, however, Artaud consented to see a gastroenterologist. In February, a series of x-rays were taken, and Artaud was assured that his condition was, indeed, no more than an abused digestion which could be set right with diet and rest. To the Thévenins, however, the doctor confided that their friend was suffering from an inoperable rectal cancer, and that he should be permitted all the opium he wanted. The end came quickly. In the early morning of March 4, 1948, the gardener at Ivry, bringing Artaud his breakfast, found the poet dead at the foot of his bed.

II

THE
SURREALIST
YEARS

The mention of Antonin Artaud's name today evokes a variety of reactions. To some, he is but the most recent incarnation of the eternally mad, misunderstood poet, while for others he is historically rooted in the Surrealist period of French letters. Most of his admirers are interested less in his literary accomplishments than in his theatrical ideas. The many different images of Artaud exist largely because, until now, only isolated portions of his work have been examined. A study of any single aspect of his work leads only to partial truths since everything he wrote is profoundly interconnected. For example: His concept of the theater becomes fully comprehensible only after the deep impression made upon him by Surrealism is understood. Throughout all his work—criticism, plays, poetry—certain themes, or leitmotifs, reoccur. It is the purpose of this book to trace the evolution of these underlying themes, so that the unity of Artaud's work and thought will emerge. It will be seen that "Artaud le Momo" is essentially the same man who complained to Rivière "I can truly say that I am not in the world, and that this is not simply an intellectual pose." (I, 40).

At the root of all of Artaud's problems and preoccupations

lay his constant struggle to "think." Throughout the 1920's he complained continually of his inability to capture and express his thoughts. A consideration of these complaints raises the understandable question: Was this inability due to physical and nervous disorders, or was it linked to the very nature of thought itself? Artaud himself (as well as many of his critics) often accepted the first of these two possibilities. In so doing, he implied that his problems were not shared by healthy men. Critics who agree with Artaud, and believe that the poet's difficulties stemmed from physiological or psychological abnormalities, usually assume that Artaud must have been mentally unbalanced in the early 20's because he showed unmistakable signs of madness at the end of his life. They attribute to this supposed mental imbalance whatever difficulties the young Artaud experienced in the thinking process. But this explanation is too pat. To begin with, the fact that Artaud began unmistakably to lose his grip on reality in the late 30's does not mean that twenty years earlier he was already so divorced from reality that he could not express himself. The facts belie this assumption: During the 1920's, Artaud could and did express himself with great clarity and insight. Further, when Artaud examines his dilemma concerning thought, it often seems that he longs to have a kind of imaginary, ideal mind. In view of this, it is not possible to maintain that a nervous disorder was the sole cause of the obstacles of which he complained when he attempted to "think." Rather, one must conclude that he desired the impossible, an "ideal" mind that has never, nor will ever, exist. In this case, Artaud's uniqueness would lie not in the difficulties he experienced in expressing his thoughts, but in the suffering that ensued when he was unable to seize and order his thoughts in the manner that he wished. To determine whether this latter conclusion is true or not, one must turn to Artaud's own analysis of his problem. At first glance, the fact that he could dissect his difficulties of expression seems to contradict his repeated assertions of failure in accomplishing that very task. Just as many of Mallarmé's best poems express his fear of not being able to create, so, too, do some of Artaud's most precise and carefully constructed descriptions of his mental state examine his professed inability to seize and express his thoughts. Aware of this seeming paradox, Artaud himself was afraid that his readers would say that the very precision of his analyses negated his claim that he could not "think." To counter this objection, Artaud insisted that his troubles were not constant and that whenever he sat down to describe them, they had all but disappeared. The fact that anyone could doubt the reality of his suffering greatly upset him. "Nothing is more detestable and painful, nothing is more anguishing for me, than doubts people have concerning the reality and the nature of the phenomena under discussion." (I, 310)

To analyze properly the difficulties Artaud experienced when he tried to capture his thoughts, it seems necessary first to define what he understood by the word "thought." This is not an easy matter since his use of the word is so fraught with ambiguities that it raises at least two major questions. When Artaud speaks of expressing his thoughts, is he referring to the act of literary creation? (If so, he would certainly not be the first writer to have faced this difficulty. Countless others have bitterly complained of their inability to express precisely what they mean; authors are in eternal pursuit of *"le mot juste."*) Or, when he refers to thought, does he use the word in the more general sense? An examination of his various statements on these questions only confuses the matter further, for different passages in his works justify varying interpretations. Although his letters to Rivière speak of thought in relation to poetic creation, in other writings Artaud discusses thought in general terms. It may be assumed that both suppositions are correct, and that the difficulties Artaud faced in the creative process are but one aspect of a greater dilemma. In addition, if the hardships he experienced in expressing his thoughts were limited to the occasions when he was engaged in poetic creation, it scarcely seems likely that the consequent suffering could have affected his life to the extent that it did. In fact, if one looks at this question from another aspect, one can see that Artaud's literary endeavors may have constituted a way of coping with the difficulties encountered when he tried to capture his thoughts. It is entirely possible that he turned to literature in the hope that, by describing his difficulties, he could exorcise himself of them; he may have hoped that the very act of writing might make it possible for him to seize and fix his thoughts. Whatever his hopes, he was bitterly disappointed, for his literary efforts only aggravated the problem. As Gaëtan Picon observes:

> Since the need for expression is born from the very impossibility of expression, from the experience of stolen words, from language which withdraws, a circle is formed: literature can only be an avowal, the story of this tragic impossibility. Language cannot cure an illness which is essentially an illness of language.[1]

And this leads to the second question: Did Artaud encounter these difficulties only when he attempted to express himself orally or in writing, or did they plague him even when he was thinking without formulating his thoughts in verbal terms? Like boxes within boxes, this query takes us to one that is even more basic: Is thought conceivable without words? Ever since the ancient Greeks, men have wondered whether or not language was necessary for the formulation of thought. Despite all past and current scientific

explorations of the mind, we are no closer today to unani-
mous agreement on this question than we have ever been.
Although Artaud's views regarding this age-old dilemma are
far from consistent, more often than not he implies that
thought *can* exist without words. In a letter to Jacques
Rivière, he distinguishes between thought and its embodiment in words:

> I suffer from a frightful illness of the mind. My thought
> abandons me at every step—from the simple fact of thought
> to the external fact of its materialization in words. Words,
> forms of phrases, inner directions of thought, simple reac-
> tions of the mind—I am in constant pursuit of my intellec-
> tual being. Whenever *I can seize a form,* however imperfect
> it may be, I hold it fast out of fear of losing the entire
> thought. (I, 20)

Clearly, for Artaud an elemental thought process ("the simple fact of thought") exists before thoughts are formulated
verbally, before "materialization" into words. This basic
process deals with "forms" which must be seized and cap-
tured by the mind. Since these forms are at the base of
thoughts, Artaud must grasp any form, however fragmentary
it may be, in order not to lose the thought. By distinguishing between the forms and the mind, Artaud makes it clear
that his conception of the mind is resolutely Cartesian. He
images the mind as a kind of empty box which must order
its content (the forms) in a rational way. His conviction that
his mind is lucid and coherent, but that it lacks inner substance or content, reflects the traditional Cartesian distinction between the mind and what it contains. Artaud's mind
is constantly in search of its content, for it cannot grasp
the fleeting and elusive forms. "My reason is untouched,
sharper than ever, it is the object to which I might apply
it that I lack, an inner substance." (I, 298)

In an important letter to Soulié de Morant, a doctor who cared for him in 1932, Artaud carries his distinction between thought and words even further. He indicates that these forms are independent not only of his mind, but of his very thoughts. The "thought" thereby becomes no more than an empty mold devised by the mind in its efforts to seize these forms.

> My mind . . . sees itself stripped of the continuity of its inner life to such a degree that the images, which are born when the subconscious joins them together and is automatically about to shape them—these images, representations and forms—*take delight* in teasing the mind by disappearing and breaking down before they reach their end, [thereby] maddening the thought which wants to seize them. (I, 311)

Artaud believed that these forms (which he also called "images" and "representations") are ordered by the subconscious before they reach the domain of the mind proper. The mind is stripped of the "continuity" of its inner life precisely because the fragmentary nature of these forms is such as to render impossible any continuous evolution of thought within the mind. But when Artaud speaks of "forms," "thoughts," and the "mind," each of which belongs to a distinct category, does it not seem as though he is constructing a highly personal picture of a brain, or, to be more exact, of a complex network of mental activities? In other words, isn't he imagining an ideal mind in which thoughts evolve by flowing smoothly from one stage to the next so that at the end of their journey they are fully formed and ready for expression? Whether or not such a mind could ever exist is not really important here. What is, however, vital, is Artaud's conviction that most men are blessed with a perfect mind in which thoughts evolve without impediments and interruptions, while his thoughts are invariably destroyed and halted in the course of their development. Some of Artaud's friends, like Rivière, who felt that the mind Artaud sought was merely a product of his imagination, suggested to him that others found it equally difficult to complete and express their thoughts. But Artaud adamantly insisted that he was more affected than anyone else, that these mental interruptions (which he refers to, variously, as "ruptures," "fissures," and "miscarriages") occurred more often to him than to anyone else. Furthermore, he asserted that other men's brains were able to hide these ruptures, while his brain was affected to a degree where it could no longer function. By "brain," Artaud appears to embrace the whole of conscious activity.

> The objection has often been made to me that these ruptures in thought, these stumblings in intellectual manifestations occur . . . to everyone. This is true, but there is a difference in quality and degree: the halt does not affect consciousness and its manifestation to the same degree. Even then, it is as if one of the links of the chain gives in, while with me it is the complete chain. The rupture momentarily destroys all consciousness. The automatic reflex of the brain which covers up these losses in others, does not cover them up in me since its very *mechanism* is affected and its functioning is stopped. (I, 317–318)

These ruptures and interruptions can occur at any time in the evolution of his thoughts. In fact, as he writes to Rivière, the fragmentary nature of his poems is due to the fact that at each level of thought, at each stage in the development of these forms, he loses control of what is happening in his mind.

> This scattered quality of my poems, these formal flaws, this constant sagging of my thought, must not be attributed to a lack of practice or control of the instrument I wielded,

[or to a lack] of *intellectual development,* but to a central collapse of the soul, to a sort of erosion of thought both essential and fleeting; to the momentary non-possession of the material gains of my development; to the abnormal separation of the elements of thought (the impulse to think, at each of the terminal stratifications of thought, including all the stages, all the bifurcations of thought and form). (I, 25)

Although his thoughts are halted at every stage of their development, interruptions become increasingly acute just as he is about to express himself in words. Distinguishing between inner words and those which are voiced (or written), Artaud complains that as soon as he attempts to express an inner word it slips away from him. When his mind attempts to pronounce these words, when it wants to materialize an image or idea by putting it into definite shape, his intellectual sickness manifests itself so that "you could say it is enough for the mind to want to enjoy an inner idea or image in order for this enjoyment to be taken away—the spoken image invariably miscarries. Trying to bring an idea or an image to the exterior is even more difficult." (I, 316)

At times Artaud believed that he was not merely losing his thoughts and words, but that someone or something was deliberately attacking him and robbing him of whatever he attempted to say or write. Although he may possess all the words necessary to express a given feeling or idea, at the very moment of expression "a higher and evil will attacks the mass of feeling, and leaves me panting as if at the very threshold of life." (I, 41) Whatever or whoever the evil spirit that robs him in this way, it destroys not only his words but the very knowledge of how to talk, "the memory of devices by which one expresses oneself and which transcribe with precision the most inseparable, the most localized, the most alive modulations of thought." (I, 26) What exactly are these devices? Artaud apparently has in mind certain phrases and forms of speech which render language quasi-automatic. It is difficult to ascertain whether he really believed that his thought was being "stolen" and "attacked," or whether he used these words metaphorically. While he was undoubtedly paranoiac toward the end of his life, and desperately afraid of evil spirits, these fears are not necessarily traceable back to the 1920's.

Artaud attributed his occasional stammer to the ruptures in his thoughts. At the same time, he was certain that the stammer, in turn, increased his difficulties in grasping his thoughts. The vicious circle was complete: His desire to speak induced an outward spasm which then contracted his inner thoughts.

> This impossibility to form and pursue thoughts manifests itself by the stammering which takes hold of my outward elocution almost every time that I wish to speak. When this happens, you could say that each time my thought wants to appear, it contracts, and that this contraction inwardly thrusts down my thought and hardens it as if in a spasm. The expression, the thought, stops because the thrust is too violent. (I, 318)

Artaud, however, demanded far more than the simple completion of his thoughts: he repeatedly expressed the wish to possess a storehouse of thoughts which could be called to the surface of his mind as needed. These thoughts would be applied, with precision, to all intellectual and emotional states. "For me, *having thought* . . . means *maintaining* your thought so that you can manifest it to yourself. It [the thought] must be able to relate to all the circumstances of feeling and life. But mainly *relate to yourself.*" (I, 68) Although not yet clothed in verbal terms, these thoughts would nevertheless have a physical density, as though they existed

concretely in the deepest recesses of Artaud's being. "I am
speaking of the physical life, of the substantial life of thought
. . . I am speaking of this minimum of thinking life at its
rough state—not yet at the stage of words, but capable of
getting there if need be." (I, 68) In addition to having a
storehouse of thoughts on call, so to speak, Artaud would
like to be fully aware of these thoughts at the time he thinks
them, as if they were physical objects that he could handle
while engaged in doing something else; he wants his thoughts
to be self-conscious, to feel their own existence. But since
thoughts are not physical objects, it is evident that once
again Artaud is reaching for the impossible. For, if thought
is to be aware of itself, it cannot at the same time be concerned with exterior ideas or emotions. If it is always turned
inward, always preoccupied with its own existence, it cannot
"think" about other things. This would preclude all mental
operations. Artaud himself was aware of this fundamental
paradox: "If you always had to think about your thought,
there wouldn't be any way of thinking, of devoting yourself
over to a mental operation superior to thought proper."
(I, 273)

Artaud's intense longing for a storage fund of completed
thoughts led to a continuing sense of frustration which was
to have far-reaching consequences. The mental ruptures he
experienced, coupled with his inability to call up thoughts
at will, gave Artaud the feeling that his very *being* was escaping him. Most men separate the realm of thought from that
of being. Artaud vehemently refused to make such a distinction. It was his refusal to separate thought and being, and
not the difficulties he experienced in trying to capture his
thoughts, that make Artaud seem so abnormal. Maurice
Blanchot, one of the poet's most astute critics, has com-
mented upon Artaud's burning desire to unite thought and
being (which Blanchot calls "life").

> He does not renounce what he calls "life" (this bursting forth, this flashing vivacity), whose loss he cannot stand, which he wants to join to this thought, which, by a grandiose and frightful obstinacy, he absolutely refuses to distinguish from thought, even though thought is nothing other than the "erosion" of this life, the "emaciation" of this life, the intimacy of rupture and loss where there is neither life nor thought, but the agony of a fundamental lack.[2]

As Blanchot observes, loss of thought is intimately related to loss of being. As Artaud's thought erodes, so too does his being, giving him the sensation that his existence is seeping away. Since his sense of existence depends upon the degree to which his thoughts have been formulated, his state of being changes with the number of his thoughts that remain unfinished. "The fluctuations of my condition are usually indicated by the greater or lesser number of times that I must complain about a thought which has miscarried, and then by the degree of stratification and of evolution or development of this thought at the moment when the rupture occurred." (I, 316) Given this interdependence of thought and being, it follows that Artaud should attribute the intermittences and absences he feels in his being to the lack of continuity and development in his thoughts. Only a continuity in his thoughts can give him the sensation of true existence, of a being that is full and complete.

> Thinking for me is something else besides being not completely dead; it means being able to unite with yourself at every moment. It means never ceasing at any moment to feel yourself in your innermost being, in the unformulated mass of your life, in the substance of your reality. It means not feeling in yourself an essential hole, a vital absence; it means feeling your thought always equal to your thought, whatever may be the inadequacies of the form you are able to give it. (I, 68)

His aim is not only to be physically conscious of his thoughts so that he can actually *feel* their presence, but also to be physically aware of his being. However, since his being depends upon his thoughts, any mental absences and gaps (such that "his thought is not always equal to his thought") result in the sensation that there is a vital absence at the core of his being. Furthermore, the mental ruptures make it impossible for him to prepare a storage fund, or reservoir, of prepared words and thoughts ("sample images"). This has serious consequences: Artaud's sense of existence depends upon the degree to which he is conscious of himself. But, to achieve this necessary level of self-awareness, he must be able to express his ideas and emotions in clearly formulated accurate terms. If, however, these terms are not forthcoming, if his words cannot be summoned at will, he loses all consciousness of his being and begins to doubt his very existence.

> The lack of continuity, the lack of extension, the lack of persistence in my thoughts is thus one of the essential characteristics of my state. Now, this lack of persistence concerning some secondary manifestation of consciousness in thoughts which are more or less innocuous and uninteresting is certainly what prevents me from becoming truly and lastingly aware of what I am and of what I think . . . and also prevents me from actively keeping in my mind a certain number of sample images corresponding to my personal sensations and representations, and consequently, from becoming and staying aware of *me*. (I, 317)

Whenever Artaud speaks of being, he quickly goes on to complain of his own "lack of being"—a lack which obsessed and tormented him throughout his life. To describe this fundamental lack of being, Artaud often has recourse to metaphors of coldness and numbness, while plenitude of being, on the other hand, is expressed in terms of fire and heat. The absence of being that he experiences is seen as a "holelike absence, a sort of stark unfeeling suffering, which is like the indescribable shock of abortions." (I, 73)

Should a man complain that he is losing his being, he may appear to be talking in abstract or metaphysical terms. Artaud, however, considers such loss to be undeniably concrete and describes it in the most vivid terms. Within his head he senses a constant anguish which is like an inner "decantation"—

> like the dispossession of my vital substance
> like the physical and essential loss
> (I mean loss from the point of view of essence)
> of a sense.
>
> (I, 89)

Artaud often expresses the belief that thought is intimately related to our physical being, rather than to any intellectual or emotional states. His body is affected when his thoughts elude him:

> I feel the ground slipping out from under my thoughts, and I am forced to envisage the terms that I use without the support of their intimate meaning, or personal substratum. . . . But this erosion which affects the base of my thought . . . does not take place in the realm of unfeeling abstractions where only the higher faculties of the intelligence participate. More than the mind which stays intact, bristling with points, it is the nervous trajectory of thought which this erosion affects and subverts. This absence and this standstill are especially felt in the limbs and blood. (I, 109–110)

Elsewhere, Artaud indicates that the origin of our thought is completely physical. *"Position de la chair"* ("The Situation of the Flesh"), an article describing the relationship between man's intellect and his body, begins with Artaud's ringing declaration that "I do not separate my thought from my life." It proceeds to tell us that only those who are unaware of true life and foolishly place their faith in the power of man's intellect fail to realize the "extent to which the Sense and Knowledge of every thought is hidden in the nervous vitality of the marrow." (I, 235–236)

One cannot read Artaud's statements on thought and being without being struck by certain ambiguities. Usually, he argues that loss of thought entails loss of being. On occasion, however, he suggests exactly the reverse, complaining that his various mental activities are affected adversely because he lacks a center of being, or of life. In one such passage, apparently unaware of any contradiction, Artaud asserts that his images, or "forms," are not authentic because his true being does not play an active role in their formulation. Since his inner being does not participate in the creation of his thoughts, the latter are but a pale reflection of thoughts that he, and others, formerly experienced. Deprived of life itself, he is unable to produce valid "forms," much less completed thoughts.

> You could say that all the images and ideas that I come upon are found by accident . . . The fact is that I am no longer myself, that my authentic self is asleep. I go toward my images. I pull them out in slow bunches; they no longer come to me, nor impose themselves on me. . . . These images, whose value depends upon their authenticity, no longer have any value, since they are mere effigies, reflections or thoughts pondered over previously, or pondered over by others, not *thought* currently and personally . . . Life does not accompany, does not illuminate what I think . . . I speak of true life, essentially illumination: being, the initial spark which lights all thought—the core. I feel my core is dead. And I suffer. (I, 298–299)

Reversing his usual complaint that the interruptions in his thoughts destroy his being, in this passage Artaud asserts that his "images" (and the thoughts which evolve from them) lack validity because they are not chosen by his true being. Whatever images he does manage to entertain, he has come by accidentally, and, since they are not pertinent to him, are completely valueless. Farther along in this passage, to explain why he feels inactive and lifeless, Artaud tells us that his being is immobilized and unable to develop. "I am fixed, localized around a point which is always the same." (I, 299) Something holds him transfixed, motionless, keeping him from life itself. He tries desperately to convince us that he suffers from "an illness which affects the deepest reality of the soul, and infects its manifestations. The poison of being. A veritable *paralysis*. An illness which deprives you of speech and memory, which uproots your thought." (I, 40) He neither lives nor thinks because his being, which should be constantly moving and evolving, is static and unchanging. He complains, in turn, of two states of being with a seeming unawareness that they are mutually exclusive: on the one hand, he fears that he is paralyzed and immobile; and on the other, that his being moves so quickly it escapes him. However contradictory these two states may appear, they lead to precisely the same result: Artaud's being cannot develop in the harmonious manner necessary to attain the desired fullness of existence. He may, on occasion, attribute his illness to various causes, but the symptoms are always the same.

The sensation that he lacks a true core of being is the basis for his fear that he has no "self." Artaud uses the word "self" to describe the hard and fixed center of a man from which all the inner forces are directed. Without this core of being—around which all our inner forces coalesce—the creation of an organic and coherent work is impossible.

> I have no reason to seek images. I KNOW that I will never find my images. Nothing will arise in me which could

achieve the degree of mental hardness, of inner construction where my self could appear or recover itself. As long as I do not find my personal fulguration, an intensity of vision, a range of conceptions born with ease (I mean born and not induced and made of odds and ends), all my works will be unreliable because they will have been born under false conditions. (I, 300)

To Artaud it is obvious that the disjointed nature of his writings reflects his fragmented being. Without a coherent self, he is unable to direct his personal vision and to choose the precise images and thoughts that correspond to what he alone thinks and feels. His images, chosen accidentally and without direction, might have been selected by anyone else. Everything he creates lacks an inner necessity.

My writing is not created and does not participate in creation . . . it is made . . . for lack of something else . . . What comes out of me is drawn out as if by chance. And I could write or say something completely different from what I say or think which would portray me just as well. That is to say, just as poorly. That is to say, not at all. . . . This is serious because it is not a question of the gratuitous work of writing, or of images for images; it is a question of absolute thought, that is to say, of life. (I, 300)

Artaud's concluding sentence is noteworthy in that it reveals the extreme importance he placed on his ability to create. Given his conviction that thought and being are indissoluble, it comes as no surprise to learn that Artaud considered his writings (which compose one aspect of thought) as part of his very being. Life and literature are as inseparable as being and thought. For this reason, when Artaud complains that he cannot write he is not simply voicing the traditional complaint of the writer who cannot find the precise words to express his thought. Rather, it is the desperate cry of a man

who believes that his very being depends upon his finding
the words he needs. Rivière's suggestion that Artaud's letters
to him be published under assumed names shocked the poet.
Artaud refused to disguise the fact that whatever he wrote
formed part of his life. "Why lie, why seek to place on a
literary level a thing which is the very cry of life? Why give
an appearance of fiction to what is made up of the uneradica-
ble substance of the soul, and which is like the moan of
reality?" (I, 38) When Artaud speaks of his writings, he refers not only to his poetry or other imaginative works, but
also to his letters and essays, for in all his works he attempts
to transcribe his inner reality. As he tells us in the opening
pages of *L'ombilic des limbes,* the main function of literature is to reveal inner being.

> Here where others offer up works I do not claim to do
> anything more than show my mind.
> Life means burning up with questions.
> I cannot conceive of a work detached from life.
> I don't like detached creativity . . . Each of my works,
> each map of myself, each of the glacial blooms of my inner
> soul, dribbles over me. (I, 49)

Convinced that literature cannot be separated from existence itself, Artaud scornfully rejects any work which he regards as unrelated to the very being of its author, any book
in which abstract intellectual ideas or esthetic values pre-
dominate, any poem which fails to communicate directly
with life. The very word "literature" evokes the notion of
detached creation in his mind. For this reason, he expresses
the hope of doing away with literature and also with pure intellectuality which is equally unrelated to man's essential
existence. Thought, being, and creation must be one and
the same. "It is necessary to do away with Mind, as with
literature. I say that Mind and life communicate on every

level. I would like to write a Book which would upset men, which would be like an open door leading them where they never would have consented to go. Simply a door touching reality." (I, 50)

If literature is to be a direct transcription of life, then the words used must correspond to man's inner reality. However, as has been stated, Artaud complains unceasingly that the words he chooses do *not* correspond to his thought, and hence to his being. Not only do his words betray and distort his ideas and feelings, they actually paralyze his thought and thereby prevent him from seeking other, more accurate, words. But he has no alternative: he must use these words if he is to think at all.

All the terms that I choose in order to think are TERMS for me in the true sense of the word, veritable terminations. . . . I am truly FIXED by my terms; and if I say that I am FIXED by my terms, it means that I do not accept them as valid in my thought. I am truly paralyzed by my terms, by a series of terminations. And WHEREVER my thought may be in these moments, I can only express it through these terms, however they may contradict it, however parallel or equivocal they may be, or else be forced to stop thinking at these moments. (I, 92–93)

All could still be set right if he could only find one word from the depths of his being, one word capable of expressing his inner reality.

Sometimes I need only one word, a simple little unimportant word, to be great, to speak in the tone of the prophets. A witness-word, a precise word, a subtle word, a word which is well macerated in my marrow. Coming from me [this word] would grasp the extreme end of being, and, for everyone else, would be nothing. I am the witness, I am the only witness of myself. (I, 89)

But this one word was to escape Artaud although he sought it all his life. It would be a mistake to think that Artaud's desire to find a word coming from the marrow of his bones is metaphorical. On the contrary, it illustrates his belief that existence is above all physical in nature, and that this physical existence is literally inseparable from thought.

Thought and language must coincide as exactly as thought and existence if writing is to be a true expression of being.

> Art is the ability to bring this rhetoric to the point of crystallization necessary for it to be one with certain real intellectual and emotional modes of being. In short, the only enduring writer is the one who knows how to make this rhetoric behave as if it were thought, and not the gesture of thought. (I, 193)

The word must not "represent" or translate thought (it is not the "gesture" of thought) but be part of it. To date, Stephen Koch is the only critic to have analyzed in depth Artaud's attempt to make language coincide absolutely with states of being.

> To express himself at all, Artaud had to wrench language out of its rationalized poetic forms and put it in direct contact with a turbulent psychic flux that had not been expressed before. Artaud wishes to rely exclusively on immediate associations between impulse and physical images.[3]

To illustrate Artaud's attempt immediately to transcribe his sensations into writing, Koch chooses the following passage from *L'ombilic des limbes:*

> Yes, space produced its extreme mental padding, in which no thought was defined, none released its charge of objects. But little by little the mass churned like a slimy powerful nausea, a kind of influx of thundering blood. And the tiny roots trembling at the edge of my mental eye detached them-

selves with dizzying speed from the wind-hardened mass.
And all space trembled like a sex pillaged by the globe of
the burning sky. (I, 51)

As Koch points out, Artaud failed in his lofty attempt to
join language and being, and was able to produce only a
series of fragmented poetic visions similar to the one just
quoted. He failed to make language coincide with being, says
Koch, for a twofold reason. In the first place, the nature of
language is such that it is formal and static—each word
"fixes" states of being, ideas, emotions, etc. And, every word
is distinct from every other. Life, on the other hand, is a
continuous flux whose "moments" cannot be isolated and
fixed. Even as we wish to stop one "moment," it has already
eluded our grasp and we are faced with the next one which
is equally fleeting. Thus, how can distinct and isolated words
coincide with a never-ceasing flow of being? Secondly, since
Artaud's mental ruptures prevented a completion of his
thoughts, how could he hope to transcribe complex feelings
and ideas in verbal terms?

> Finally, the realization of Artaud's intuitively ordered chaos
> was impossible. The very idea is a contradiction, assuming
> as it does that a violent mental flux can be made ideal, and
> brought to rest, like an object. But beyond the formal in-
> capacity of language to embody this contradiction, there
> was something in Artaud's illness itself that annihilated
> thought on the verge of expression.[4]

Artaud's inability to make words coincide with his inner
being often led him to lose all faith in the power and validity
of literary creation. At such times he would condemn literature violently:

> All writing is filthy.
> People who leave the realm of obscure in order

to define whatever it is that goes on in their
heads are swine.
All literary people are swine, especially today.

(I, 95)

His rejection of literature often includes a denunciation of
language and of mind:

And I told you: no works, no language, no words, no
mind, nothing.
Nothing except a beautiful Nerve-scale.

(I, 96)

Feelings of self-estrangement also stem from Artaud's inability to find the words corresponding to his inner reality.
As we've seen, his sense of self-awareness, and hence, of existence, depends upon the degree to which he can express his
being in accurate verbal terms. When he fails to find such
terms, he is led to question the reality of his reactions to given
stimuli and experiences. This, in turn, leads to a "collapse
of the facts such that I . . . ask myself why, for example, red
(the color) is considered red and affects me as red? why do
decisions affect me like decisions and not like pain? why do
I feel pain?" (I, 319) Not only does he question the simplest
reactions, he becomes incapable of expressing the most ele-
mentary sensations. When it is cold he is incapable of making an objective statement to that effect. He is unable to say
that it is cold without the fear that what he is experiencing
(in this case, the most elemental physical reactions) will not
be accurately expressed by these few words.

If I'm asked why I can't say it ["it is cold"], I would answer
that my inner feeling concerning this fragmentary and innocuous fact does not correspond to the three simple words
that I should pronounce. And this lack of correspondence
between a physiological sensation and the emotional . . . and

intellectual awareness we have of it . . . results, when it becomes widespread, in colossal difficulties which correspond
perfectly to the loss of personality. (I, 320–321)

The lack of rapport between his sensations and the words
employed to express them causes him to doubt the reality of
the former. And this doubt leads him to question the reality
of his personality and his being.

The frustration he experiences whenever he attempts to
express an emotional or intellectual state results in a sense
of self-alienation so intense that the manifestations of his personality no longer seem to belong to him. Incapable of claiming any ideas or emotions as his own, he complains, "Neither my scream nor my fever is mine. My secondary forces,
these hidden elements of thought and soul, are disintegrating, but try to imagine how they linger on." (I, 105) Since
Artaud refuses to divorce his mental state from his physical
being, it follows that his self-estrangement should have physical symptoms. He suffers "a sensation of physical remote-
ness from myself as if I were no longer about to control my
limbs, my reflexes, or my most spontaneous mechanical reactions." (I, 311)

Other indications of Artaud's self-estrangement manifest
themselves throughout his work. He is haunted by an ever-
present sense of being two people. He is himself and, at the
same time, he is engaged in watching himself. "I know myself, and that's enough for me, and that must be enough for
me. I know myself because I am my own audience, I am the
audience of Antonin Artaud." (I, 93) Although this *"dédou-
blement"* usually indicates a state of self-alienation so extreme as to be regarded as an illness, Artaud welcomed, and
even provoked, a split personality. He deliberately sought to
identify with other people so that he could remain himself
and yet watch himself be another. The explanation for this
kind of conduct is complex and is related to Artaud's con-

stant fear that his being was escaping. One way of fixing his being, of giving himself a stable and coherent identity, would be to identify with someone else. Another's being invariably appears to us unified and coherent, while our own is elusive and lacking definite character traits. Artaud never finds within himself the immutable hardness and solidity that he sees in others.

Artaud identifies not only with other men, but with their "myth." Such a "myth" is composed of all the attributes and qualities that history and legend ascribe to a man after death. It is even more satisfying to identify with the "myth" of a man than with the man himself; since the "myth" has been fixed by history, it is less subject to change. Identifying with the "myth" of Paolo Uccello, Artaud sees himself as Uccello while remaining conscious of himself as Artaud. In Sartrean terms, he becomes both subject and object, creator and created:

> I am like a theatrical character who has the ability to con-
> template himself and to be, at times, a pure and simple
> mental abstraction, and at others, the inventor and the ani-
> mator of this mental creature. While still alive, he would
> have the ability to deny his existence and to hide from the
> pressure of his antagonist. (I, 209)

By identifying with another, Artaud not only confers upon himself a density of being, he also escapes from his own problems. He becomes the person with whom he identifies: "I am such as I see myself." (I, 209) The sense of self-aware-ness he so desires is only attained when he can watch him-self as he would another person. He makes a further demand: to effect the identification without a conscious awareness of what he is doing. Attributing this desire to Paolo Uccello, he states that the painter "explores an unthinkable problem: to make up his mind, as if it were not he who was doing so . . . To keep the advantages of his personal judgment while alienating the personal quality of this judgment. To see himself and be unaware that it is he who sees himself." (I, 205)

Artaud's sense of self-estrangement is accompanied by the feeling that he is alienated from reality. Completely isolated from the world, he suffers states of mind "where the simplest, most commonplace reality does not reach me, where the instant pressure of normal reality does not get through to me, where I do not even reach the necessary level of my life." (I, 218) The sense of alienation is manifested in his work by a number of recurrent metaphors. He speaks often of panes of glass, and of labyrinths, which bar him from reality. While he is able to see the world, access to it is blocked. Although Artaud identifies with Uccello in the essays devoted to the painter, in several passages he speaks only of himself. He describes the alienation from reality experienced by Artaud–Uccello, as well as his, Artaud's, own sense of estrangement. After we learn that Uccello is "struggling in the midst of a vast mental tissue where he has lost all the roads to his soul," Artaud goes on to complain that, like the painter, *he* is fighting to regain contact with reality. "There is also Antonin Artaud. But an Antonin Artaud in labor, who is on the other side of all this mental glass and who is making every effort to think of himself in another place." (I, 55) On occasion, the pane of glass that separates him from the world moves into his brain. Here, too, the glass permits him to glimpse outer reality but prevents any real contact. In *"La nuit opère"* ("Night Works"), one of Artaud's early poems, he observes:

> Glasses and bellies collide
> life is transparent
> in glassy skulls.
> (I, 227)

Far more powerful than the metaphor of coated glass is
that of the mummy. Artaud's double sense of alienation—
from self and from reality—leads to the conviction that he
is removed from life even while he remains aware of it. He
likens himself to a mummy which is dead, but which is pre-
served in such a way that it continues to "live." In his *Correspondance de la momie"* Artaud describes this mummy-
state experience, this continual life-in-death.

> This flesh no longer touching itself in life,
> this tongue which can no longer go beyond its shell,
> this voice which no longer travels through the roads of
>   sound,
> this hand which has forgotten more than the gesture of
>   taking,
> and no longer succeeds in gauging the space where it will
> complete its grip,
> finally this brain in whose lines conceptions are no longer
> defined,
> all these things which form my mummy of live flesh give
>   god
> an idea of the void into which the necessity of being born
> has placed me.
> My life is not complete, but neither has my death been
> absolutely aborted.
>
> (I, 241)

Artaud was drawn to the subject of mummies not only because he saw a parallel between his state and theirs; he was
also interested in the ancient Egyptian religion and, in fact,
quite familiar with the Egyptian Book of the Dead.

The robot could be called the modern counterpart of the
mummy: it does not live and yet it is "alive" in that it performs certain automatic gestures. So, it is not surprising to
find Artaud comparing himself to a robot—one, however,
who is aware of the tragedy of his condition. Condemning

God for having determined him without his consent or participation, Artaud is bitter in his complaint:

> This God has disposed of me to the point of absurdity; he has kept me alive in a void of negations and stubborn self-disavowals. He has destroyed everything in me, down to the least outgrowth of conscious, sentient life. He has reduced me to being a walking robot, but a robot who can feel the rupture of his unconscious. (I, 223)

The loss of thought and being, as well as feelings of alienation, inevitably affect Artaud's relationship with the world. His lack of a sense of being, and the absence of a central core within himself which he could call his "self," make for a feeling of vulnerability in dealing with external objects and forces. If he is nothing but absence and emptiness, how is he to preserve his being when confronted with the encroaching materiality of outer reality? He clings desperately to hard objects which promise to replace the moving quicksand of his being. Drawn to anything which appears firm enough to protect him against the world, he shies away from the soft and viscous. In general, Artaud equates hardness with all that is necessary and determined, and softness with things formless and uncontrolled. He desires desperately to be self-determined, to be capable of choosing his thoughts and directing his being without exterior pressures. It is his own will that must control his life, his being, and his thought. Bitterly resentful that he has been determined by forces outside himself, he decries the fact that he can do nothing to alter the course of his life. Suicide attracts him because it, at least, seems to be an act of self-determination. "By suicide, I would reintroduce my pattern into nature. For the first time I would give things the shape of my will. I would free myself of the conditioned reflexes of my organs which correspond so poorly to my inner self. Life for me would no longer be an absurd accident where I think what I am told to think." (I, 221) But he soon realizes that the victory apparently offered by suicide is merely an illusion. In taking his own life he will probably be effectuating some over-all, prearranged design; so, he can no more determine his death than he can his life. His inability to exercise his will and control his life means that he is no longer a man but a mere object. "It is certainly abject to be created and live and to feel oneself irrevocably predestined down to the furthest corners of oneself, down to the most *unthought of* ramifications of one's being. We are only trees after all and it is probably written in some nook or other of my family tree that I shall kill myself on a given day." (I, 222) Although he appears to be alive, he is nothing more than an inanimate object. "I am made of blood, obviously I am made of blood. But I cannot see myself right now. I do not think of myself as being alive. I am such as I was made, that's all." (I, 208)

The absence of hardness within him is such that he is readily suffocated and crushed by the outside world. An incident recounted by Anaïs Nin illustrates how intensely Artaud feared suffocation. She and Artaud were observing a dog in the midst of digging a hole. Artaud suddenly broke into a cold sweat and cried, "Stop him! He is making a tunnel. I will be caught inside it and suffocate to death. Stop him! I can't breathe."[5] Images of strangulation and asphyxiation occur repeatedly throughout Artaud's work, from his very first writings to the poems created shortly before his death. In *"Fragments d'un journal d'enfer"* he complains that at the center of his being he is strangling. "This knot of life where the emission of thought clings. A knot of all-permeating asphyxiation." (I, 105)

In those moments when Artaud's being is crushed, his mind is slowly strangled. The mind suffocates not because it has too many images and thoughts, but because it is empty and immobile—it expires like a candle in an airless room:

> There is an acid and turbid anguish, as powerful as a knife . . . an anguish where the mind strangles and cuts itself—and kills itself.
> It consumes nothing that doesn't belong to it, it is born of its own asphyxiation.
> It is a *congealing* of the marrow, an absence of mental fire, a lack of circulation of life. (I, 72)

The vacuum in the mind which leads to its suffocation also provokes paralysis. Lacking an essential flow of thoughts and the momentum which would enable it to pursue its activities, the mind becomes immobile and frozen. Artaud suffers a "lack of normal vitality which prevents me from keeping track of my ideas . . . and from reviewing at will my opinions and decisions." (I, 321–322) This paralysis attacks his entire being, rendering him totally incapable of directing his thought and even his existence.

> Paralysis overtakes me and increasingly prevents me from finding myself. I no longer have any support, any base. . . . My thought can no longer go where my emotion and the images arising in me push it. I feel castrated down to my slightest impulses. . . . You must understand that it is truly the living man in me who is affected and that this paralysis which suffocates me is at the center of my everyday personality. (I, 107)

It is not by accident that Artaud uses the word "castrated" in describing his paralysis. Accompanying the sensations of alienation and suffocation are definite sexual fears.

Artaud's view of sex is clearly polarized; the lines separating masculinity from femininity are hard and fast. Solidity, rationality, and dominance are traits of the male; viscosity and formlessness are characteristics of the female. Matter, the shapeless female principle, often suffocates and engulfs the rational masculine mind. One of the best of Artaud's early poems, *"Avec moi dieu-le-chien"* ("On my side god-the-dog"), forcefully suggests this fundamental struggle between mind and matter, or masculinity and femininity. A tongue, representing the masculine principle, tries to pierce the earthly crust of soft matter which threatens to subdue and annihilate it.

> On my side god-the-dog, like a shaft
> its tongue pierces the crust
> of the earth's vaulted double
> dome which itches it.
>
> (I, 53)

But the earth, the horrible rotten earth, succeeds in crushing the tongue; god-the-dog, meanwhile, it metamorphosed into god-the-bitch.

> Under the breasts of the hideous earth
> god-the-bitch has withdrawn,
> away from breasts of earth and frozen water
> which rot her hollow tongue.
>
> (I, 53)

Does the hollow tongue symbolize the core of emptiness which Artaud experiences at the center of his thoughts and being? Even if this interpretation seems overly ingenious, the tongue remains an interesting symbol for its shape evokes the phallus, while it also plays an important role in the formation of words and thoughts. And, Artaud apparently views sexual virility and the ability to think rationally as related activities. This is particularly clear in the poem *"La nuit opère"* in which it is suggested that the poet's sexual powers and his thought desert him simultaneously.

> On all the bars of the earth
> pile up uprooted glasses
> the poet feels his thought
> and his sexual organ abandons him
>   (I, 227)

In another passage, mysterious forms threaten both his ability to think and his virility.

> I feel that the despair brought to me by these terrifying advancing forms is alive. It creeps in at this knot of life beyond which extend the paths of eternity. It is truly an eternal separation. They slide their knife into this center where I feel myself a man, they cut the vital ties which join me to the dream of my lucid reality. (I, 108)

It can be readily understood that a man who longed in vain to determine his own existence should also suffer fears of sexual impotence. Such fears are manifest throughout his work. In one of his articles on Uccello, Artaud transfers his feelings of impotence to the Florentine painter. Uccello appears sexually inferior to Brunelleschi, a rival for the affections of Uccello's wife. Artaud's comparison of the two men belittles the painter by pointing out his sexual inadequacy: "Paul of the Birds has an imperceptible voice, the bearing of an insect, a dress too big for him. Brunelleschi, on the other hand, has a sonorous and full-bodied stage voice; he resembles Dante." (I, 210)

The threat of sexual impotence, and the anguish experienced when confronted by shapeless female matter, inevitably affect everything Artaud writes on the subject of sex. Physical love is usually depicted as repulsive and criminal. In the tale entitled *"La vitre d'amour"* ("The Windowpane of Love") Artaud describes his relationship with a Kafkaesque tavern maid: "It was a sky of protesting sin, a sin held back

at confession, one of these sins which burdens the conscience
of priests, a true theological sin." (I, 151) And the woman
herself becomes progressively more unattractive: "She was
a maid, as in a Hoffmanlike tavern, but a shabby dissolute
little maid, a filthy and unwashed maid." (I, 151) *"Rêve"*
("Dream"), a hallucinatory work, pictures an orgy during
which Artaud makes love to his sister. Following the incestuous act, he and his companions assume long dresses to
conceal their sin as his mother enters in the habit of an
abbess.

Sadism and sexual violence are particularly evident in Artaud's early scenarios. The first of these, *Le jet de sang*, depicts a multitude of scorpions welling up from beneath the
skirts of a nursemaid who also nourishes strange shiny beasts
in her sexual parts. *La révolte du boucher (The Butcher's
Revolt)* presents a butcher who spreads a woman out on a
table as if to dismember her and is halted by an enjoining
voice: "I've had enough of cutting up meat without eating
it." (II, 51) Sadism of this sort is also found in *Les 32*. The
"32" of the title refers to the number of women destroyed
by a vampire. Artaud's only realized scenario, *La coquille
et le clergyman*, exhibits an impotent clergyman who pur-
sues a woman and, after attempting to lacerate her breasts,
strangles what appears to be her double. Rounding off this
assemblage of horrors is *La pierre philosophale (The Philosopher's Stone)*, in which a doctor pauses in the course of
sadistic experiments in order to make love.

All of these interlocking themes—Artaud's fear of impotence and castration, his repulsion at the thought of sex, the
need to dominate himself and others—are present in two
remarkable articles devoted to Peter Abelard, the medieval
French scholar who fell in love with, and secretly married,
his pupil Heloise. Castrated by assassins hired by Heloise's
uncle, Abelard became a monk at the Abbey of Saint-Denis.

The Abelard envisaged by Artaud is, of course, different in all respects from the man who wrote the world-famous love letters to Heloise. Identifying with Abelard, Artaud attributes his own fears and obsessions to the medieval cleric. Artaud–Abelard suffocates while his brain gradually disintegrates. "Life contracted before his eyes. Entire areas of his brain were rotting." (I, 129) Mocked by everything firm and masculine, he trembles before women whose hardness and strength only emphasize his impotence and weakness. "I can't do anything if I am a summit where the highest masts use breasts in place of sails, while women feel their sexual organs become as hard as pebbles." (I, 129) For Artaud–Abelard, the sexual act is accompanied by blasphemy and ugliness; while making love, Abelard shouts, "Your God is nothing but cold lead, fertilizer of limbs, whorehouse of eyes, virgin of the stomach, dairy of the sky." (I, 132) If this description of love leaves a reader untouched, there is still the revolting figure of Heloise. After seeing Abelard emasculated, she appears in the nude. "Her skull is white and milky, her breasts suspicious, her legs skinny, her teeth sound like the rustle of paper. She is stupid. And here you have the wife of Abelard the eunuch." (I, 133) Hater of women and sex, Artaud could hardly have identified himself with any character more antithetic than Abelard, the romantic and passionate lover.

While the historical Abelard was castrated by his wife's uncle, Artaud–Abelard is emasculated by Heloise herself. Playing with the words "sex-sextant," Artaud describes Heloise's sex: "She also had this thing in the form of a naval sextant, around which all magic turns and grazes, this thing like a sheathed sword." (I, 130) By employing the image of a sheathed sword, Artaud reveals that his hatred of sexuality is related to a fear of castration. Although Heloise may appear magically alluring, she is, like all women, fundamentally corrupt and corrupting. "Her body is white but blemished, for no woman's belly is pure. Their skin is the color of mildew." (I, 136) Even Heloise is vaguely aware of the obscenity inherent in sex: she regrets not having "in place of her belly, a wall like the one she leaned against when Abelard crushed her with his obscene dart." (I, 137) Appropriately enough, Artaud ends his narration of the Abelard–Heloise tragedy by averring his desire for sexual abstinence and purity. Nearly twenty years later, Artaud was still haunted by the figure of Abelard. Anaïs Nin recounts that even in the asylum Artaud was pursued by "a monk who is castrated and who sometimes takes the form of a woman."[6]

In the two articles dealing with Heloise and Abelard, Artaud's desire to dominate himself emerges in a curiously ambiguous manner. Contrary to what one might expect, Artaud–Abelard welcomes the fact that the sexual act, by rendering him weak and helpless, deprives him of self-control he might otherwise possess. This contradicts what he says elsewhere of his wish to take charge of himself. The only satisfactory explanation for this contradiction appears, at first glance, paradoxical: Artaud welcomes the fact that he is no longer responsible for himself precisely because of his incapacity to determine and govern his own being. Once deprived of any possibility of control, he enjoys a deep sense of relief. Indeed, Artaud–Abelard is glad that in Heloise's presence he cannot even attempt to dominate himself, and that he becomes nothing more than a mere object in her mind. "I am the needle running through her thought and her soul accepts and admits the needle. I myself am better in my needle than all the others in their beds, because in my bed I turn the thought and the needle over in the folds of her sleeping cocoon." (I, 131) Heloise relieves him of his problems and fears. Otto Hahn, an existentialist critic, has remarked that Artaud "lets himself be manipulated because Heloise takes charge of his body, demands no concessions, accepts him entirely."[7] In this way, Artaud is reduced to nothing more than an inanimate object; he is merely "there." Not only is his being definite and coherent, but his thoughts are finally fixed since there can exist no possibility of change so long as he remains an object. However, those thoughts are now flat and shallow, for they exist only insofar as they can be observed by another. And no one else can see into the depths of a man's thoughts. Free from the loss of thought and being, both having achieved a thing-like rigidity, Artaud's mind ceases to torture him.

> The fact is that at this moment Abelard enjoys his mind. He enjoys it fully. He no longer thinks of himself to the right or to the left. He is there. Everything happening in him is his. And in him, at this moment, things are happening. Things which release him from seeking himself. That's the main point. He no longer needs to stabilize his atoms. . . . He is really there. He is there like a living medal, like a bush which has turned into metal. (I, 131, 132)

By repudiating all responsibility for his own existence, Artaud is relieved of the necessity to solve his problems. Only at this moment, when he assumes the being of an inanimate object, does he approach a semblance of inner peace.

Other passages also reveal Artaud's ambivalence regarding the desire to control his life. In a letter addressed to a clairvoyant ("Lettre à une voyante"), he shows a thorough awareness of the paradoxical nature of his reactions. He begins by telling us that normally he needs to feel he has a determining role in life. Once in front of the fortuneteller, however, this attitude undergoes a sudden change. "I no longer feel the need to be powerful or vast; the fascination that she exerts upon me is more violent than my pride . . .

I am ready to relinquish everything in front of her: pride, free will, intelligence. Especially intelligence." (I, 126) Elsewhere, he asserts that all men, like himself, have been deprived of free will and self-determination. The vast majority of them, however, refuse to accept this fundamental truth and, consequently, fail to understand that "it is better to be in a state of perpetual abdication toward your mind. It is a better, more normal state for man, one which is better suited to our grim human condition and to man's grim claim that he has free will." (I, 219) It would appear that Artaud accepts with relief, if not joy, the realization that he is not free. When he is convinced that the struggle for control is useless, he ceases to fight with a deep sense of peace. He is more than thankful to yield in a hopeless battle.

Artaud's attempts to deal with the manifold problems flowing from his loss of thought and being led him to investigate various domains of art, philosophy, and religion. His attraction to the plastic arts, especially painting, is at least partially attributable to his difficulties. Artaud was certain that painters were able to "fix" their thoughts and images in space, unlike writers and poets who must contend with the elusive nature of language. Also, painters are not faced with the need to make words correspond to inner reality; emotions and perceptions are transcribed in plastic terms. If Artaud could only fix his thoughts in space, he would finally have his desired storage fund of ready-made thoughts.

Drawn, as he was, to painters who worked in clear, solid forms, Artaud devoted two articles to Uccello, among the first artists to experiment with linear perspective. Addressing himself to the Florentine master, Artaud makes it clear that he envies Uccello the painter's ability to order thoughts

spatially, while he, a poet, must deal with ephemeral impulses which cannot be grasped and be expressed in solid
forms. "May you be very happy, you who have had a rocky
and earthy preoccupation with depth." (I, 139) Expressing
impulses and feelings spatially, Uccello communicates with
others while Artaud loses himself in the labyrinth of his own
mind. Although Uccello may embark upon a project with
shadowy images and unformed sensations, he is able ultimately to render them in concrete form: the very nature of
his work spares him from the threat of incomplete thoughts.
Once again, Artaud addresses the painter: "You were born
with a mind as hollow as mine, but you were able to fix this
mind on something even less than the imprint or the birth
of an eyelash. By a hair's breadth you are dangling over a
frightening abyss and yet you are eternally separated from
it." (I, 140)

A contemporary painter who was greatly admired by
Artaud is Balthazar Klossowski de Rola, more commonly
known as Balthus. A close friend of Artaud's, Balthus was
responsible for the costumes and scenery of Artaud's production of Les Cenci. Although his paintings reflect the influence
of Surrealism, Balthus, like Uccello, places great emphasis on
form and depth. In his references to Balthus (as in the case of
Uccello), Artaud makes no secret of his envy of the painter's
ability to control and dominate thought impulses by projecting them onto canvas. In Balthus' work, every idea assumes a concrete form so that even portraits suggest various concepts and attitudes. All is conveyed pictorially: Material forms embody ideas and thoughts, thereby dispensing
with the need for conceptual language. And, as Otto Hahn
observes, "If Artaud is drawn to painting, it is because the
pictorial language transforms emotion into objects and objects into emotion. The immobile image is only expression

and spirituality. You don't need to understand anything, but
only to feel the spiritual content."[8]

Far more important than Artaud's attraction to painting
and painters was his association with Surrealism, surely the
most important literary movement of the first half of this
century. Although Artaud was a full-fledged Surrealist for
only a few years—from 1924 to 1927—the influence of the
movement permeates so much of his work that it is difficult
to determine to what extent Surrealist tenets reinforced his
own basic tendencies, and to what degree his ideas were
shaped through affiliation with these painters and writers. As
one might have expected, Artaud welcomed those aspects of
Surrealism which seemed to offer him some means of justifying, or of solving, his problems. He was drawn to the Surrealists' rejection of rational, logical thought, and to their
quest for a reality beyond that of the everyday world. Convinced that our conventional perception of the world had
to be destroyed in order to find this reality, the Surrealists
turned to drugs, dreams, automatic writing, and hallucina-
tion. Even madness was regarded as an acceptable way of
furthering this process of destruction.

The Surrealists' condemnation of Western society's traditional reliance on so-called logical thought appealed to Artaud partly because of his own inability, real or imagined,
to express his thought impulses in rational terms. One issue
of *la Révolution surréaliste* contains a number of anonymous
articles (since ascribed to Artaud) decrying the faith Occidental society places in reason and rationality. One such
article, entitled *"L'activité du bureau de recherches sur-
réalistes"* ("Activities of the Office of Surrealistic Research"),
proclaimed the Surrealists' desire for a revolution which
would destroy and disqualify logic and effect a reclassifica-
tion of institutions "according to a deeper and subtler order

which is inexplicable by means of ordinary reasoning." (I, 268) In another article, Artaud warns the Establishment "look out for your logic—you do not know to what point our hatred of logic can take us." (I, 252)

Artaud shared the Surrealist dream of establishing contact with another reality, one far surpassing the world of ordinary logic and natural law. Such contacts could be effected only in "surrealistic" states during which a man apparently loses control of his being but, in fact, experiences a different kind of control, one that "prevents contact with ordinary reality and allows these subtler and more rarefied contacts. . . . I envision a well-worn soul, brim-stoned and phosphorized by these contacts, as the only acceptable state of reality." (I, 86) The Surrealists turned to drugs, among other things, to free themselves from the logic of normal reality. Artaud had always depended on drugs to subdue physical pain, but now he was able to justify this need by asserting that drugs "liberate and sharpen" the mind, enabling it to soar beyond the confines of the everyday world. He goes on to say that from the standpoint of normal reality it matters little whether the revelations produced by drugs are true or false. As in the case of death, drugs clear the path to a reality which is infinite in nature and beyond the realm of matter. For this reason, Artaud calls drugs the "closest and most useful aides of death." (I, 121)

To the world of drugs, and the hallucinations they provoke, must be added that of dreams. These play an important role in the Surrealist mythos, for Artaud and the others believed that they too allowed us to transcend the limitations of the ordinary world. "I give myself to the fever of dreams in order to derive new laws." (I, 239) He has nothing but scorn for those who do not understand the value of dreams. "All those who dream without grieving for their dreams, without suffering from a feeling of unbearable nostalgia after plunging down into a fertile subconscious, are swine. Dreaming is true. All dreams are true." (I, 121)

Artaud felt that dreams could enlighten us about true reality because of their capacity to reveal our subconscious. Many Surrealists, in fact, hoped to make contact with another reality not only through the changes in our psyche provoked by drugs and dreams, but through the intervention of human love and the subconscious. In these respects, however, Artaud was radically at odds with the others, particularly Breton, whose very name invariably brings to mind the image of Woman. In all Breton's books, from *Nadja* (1928), which paints the portrait of an alluring, mysterious female endowed with supernatural powers, to *L'amour fou* (1937) and *Arcane 17* (1945), Breton stresses the vital importance of women and love. He believed that woman could effect man's spiritual regeneration by enabling him to discern the secrets of the universe. Extolling love in all its aspects, Breton refused to distinguish between its physical and spiritual sides. "It is quite certain that physical love is one with spiritual love."[9] The power of love can be fully understood and appreciated only when man liberates his sexual desires which have for centuries been repressed by fears and taboos. Artaud's own fears rendered him totally unable to accept Breton's ideas on the role of human sexuality and love. No one could be further removed from Breton than the Artaud who abhorred sex and women, the Artaud who longed to be chaste.

Breton also exalted the power of love in the belief that it could free our buried subconscious forces which would then rise up and destroy society's artificial, life-constricting barriers and restrictions. Convinced that the recesses of man's mind had to be brought to light before he could recover his lost, or repressed, psychic forces, Breton asserted, "Let us remember that the idea of Surrealism simply leads to the total recuperation of our psychic force by a means which is none other than a dizzying descent into ourselves, a systematic illumination of hidden places, and perpetual walking in the midst of a forbidden zone."[10] Artaud's attitude toward the subconscious is far more ambivalent and complicated than are his sentiments regarding women and sex. At times he gives the impression that he would like nothing better than to believe in the value of his subconscious; at one point he explains that he was attracted to Surrealism because it gave promise of permitting him to enter into contact with a profound reality through the release of repressed instincts. "Surrealism has never been anything for me but a new sort of magic. Imagination, dreams, all this intense liberation of the subconscious—the goal of which is to bring to the soul's surface all that is usually hidden." (I, 287)

However, passages such as this, which manifest Artaud's desire to free his subconscious instincts, are not quite as convincing as those revealing his fears of these very same instincts. It is not always clear what Artaud truly fears. These instincts may appear menacing because they threaten to usurp any self-control he does manage to assert. It is also possible that he associates his subconscious with his own abhorred sexuality. One passage in particular illustrates both these fears (obviously interrelated), expressing, as it does, Artaud's belief that his subconscious forces render his mind incapable of imposing a rational and coherent order on thought impulses.

> It has been a long time since I had any control over my mind, and my subconscious rules me with impulses which come from the depths of my nervous rages and from the whirling of my blood. Hurried and rapid images send only

words of anger and blind hate to my mind, but are over as quickly as stabs of a knife or flashes of lightning in a congested sky. (I, 107–108)

His conscious mind is compelled to submit to his subconscious which, in turn, is dominated by his physical being, his "nervous rages." His subconscious, like his thought impulses, has its roots in the "marrow of his bones." From the images Artaud evokes it is clear that his subconscious instincts do not merely obstruct his thought processes but threaten to destroy him, like the "stabs of a knife."

What may be considered the single most important aspect of Artaud's affiliation with Surrealism has not yet been mentioned. This is the attitude of the Surrealists toward literature and language. The similarities between Breton's ideas and those of Artaud on the nature and function of literary creation are striking. Once again, it is impossible to say whether Artaud was deeply influenced by Breton and the others or whether their demands served to corroborate his own ideas. In any case, Breton, like Artaud, insisted that literature could not be separated from the deepest layers of life. To make being and literature coincide, the Surrealists practiced what they called "automatic writing." A somnambulistic or trancelike state would be induced, and the subject would then attempt to record the thoughts and images that came to his mind. This, without the intervention of the rational mind which normally orders everything in "literary" fashion. In this manner the Surrealists tried to rid themselves of the distortions language usually imposes upon our immediate (and disordered) sensations and fragmentary thoughts. As Maurice Blanchot observes, "Literature is banished, but language becomes one with the pure moment of consciousness."[11] The great importance the Surrealists placed upon automatic writing may be seen in Breton's early definition of Surrealism:

A pure psychic automatism by which one proposes to express, either verbally or in writing, or in any other way, the real functioning of thought; dictation by thought, in the absence of any control exercised by reason, and without any esthetic or moral considerations.[12]

Their demand that writers express man's inner reality, which is instinctual, led Artaud and Breton to denounce any literature which was under the influence of the intellect. Logic and reason, they said, only distorted essential truths, since reality cannot be explained rationally. Breton dismissed novels because they belonged to the realm of reason and logical analysis. All of this, however, raises a question that has already been examined in regard to Artaud himself. Were Breton and the others seeking the impossible? For one thing, as has been stated, any attempt to express directly man's inner psychic flow was doomed to failure because of the static nature of language itself. Furthermore, all literature as we know it would disappear if logic and rational coherence were destroyed and writers portrayed no more than fragmentary visions, however poetic, of their inner states of being. The irony is that the Surrealists turned to literature for the purpose of condemning it.

The Surrealists' conviction that literature should be a direct expression of life led them to a re-evaluation of the nature of language. Language assumed a primary role for them, since they believed that the words we used both reflected and promulgated our false conception of reality. Breton and Artaud were equally contemptuous of the depths to which ordinary language had sunk. Convinced that our language was intimately linked to a decadent bourgeois society, Breton declared that everyday language perpetuated outworn traditions and conceptions. "Words are likely to group themselves according to particular affinities, [thereby] re-creating the world in accordance with its old pattern at every mo-

ment."[13] In his first "Manifesto of Surrealism," Breton called
for a new language which would both reveal the profound
depths of man's being and also change our perception of
reality. "Language has been given to man so that he can
use it surrealistically." [14] Nearly thirty years later this conviction was unchanged. Reviewing the aims and accomplishments of the Surrealist movement, he asserted in 1953 that
Surrealism had wanted to "restore language to its true life."
Breton was unceasing in his condemnation of everyday language because of its inability to express and evoke fundamental states of being. "We pretend not to notice that . . .
the logical mechanism of the sentence appears more and
more incapable of releasing the emotional shock in man
which actually gives some value to his life." [15] Artaud's rejection of traditional language was, if anything, far more
heated than Breton's. In one of the anonymous articles
originally published in *la Révolution surréaliste,* Artaud
declares war on ordinary language because it expresses only
the most superficial aspects of human life. True language,
on the other hand, reveals the most fundamental human
substratum which is irrational and logically inexplicable.

Artaud's desire to destroy logical language is so intense
that it often seems of no consequence to him whether the
new language he seeks is comprehensible or not. At one
point he even maintains that the principal function of language is not communication but the illumination of one's
very being. As spokesman for the Surrealists, he defiantly
asserts they no longer care whether the world understands
them or not: "The break between us and the world is well
established. We speak not to be understood, but to our inner
selves. With plowshares of anguish, with the keen edge of
a stubborn obstinacy, we reverse and tear into thought." (I,
269) Despite ringing statements of this sort, many of Artaud's
works betray desperate longings to communicate. As Nicola

Chiaromonte observes, the letters Artaud wrote to Rivière show not only a wish to be understood, but a desire for "a unique and privileged place in the world of letters."[16] It is frequently clear that Artaud wishes that some men, if not everyone, will understand him. In one passage he asserts that he is addressing himself to those who share his inability to express thoughts. But even if it were true that he is writing only for those who are "discredited by words and speech, the pariahs of Thought," it is to be noted that he is still writing for *someone*. Not only does Artaud want to communicate with others, on more than one occasion he gives the impression that he would welcome a sympathetic response. His repeated assertions that being understood was of little moment to him could only have derived from the despair that overwhelmed him when he attempted to express his thoughts. Finally, the very fact that Artaud and Breton wanted to transform language showed that they cared, and cared deeply, about communication.

Once they had decided that ordinary language had to be discarded, Artaud and the others were faced with the problem of creating a new language or of forcing our old one to undergo a metamorphosis. In addition to automatic writing, one of the important ways in which they proposed to change language, and thereby transform our vision of reality, was through the use of the "poetic image." Such an "image" is created by joining things or qualities normally quite unrelated to one another, entities that do not normally find themselves in any sort of proximity. Through the "image" the Surrealists hoped to permit us insights into mysterious and inexplicable phenomena, allowing us to view reality in a wholly new way. "We are infinitely sensitive to a special light —*a light of the image*—which has sprung forth from bringing together two terms in a way which is somehow fortuitous."[17] The "image" is not composed consciously or de-

liberately; in fact, the rational mind plays a completely
passive role. "The two terms of the image are not derived
from each other by the mind in the hope of producing a
spark . . . they are the simultaneous products of the activity
which I call surrealist. Reason merely observes and appre-
ciates the luminous phenomenon."[18] Artaud professed great
faith in the power of poetic images to bring us closer to hidden reality. Images, evoking each other by their own laws of
association, can teach us more about the fundamental nature
of our being than discursive language, for they speak from
the hidden depths of the subconscious. "In the elevated domain of images, true illusion (material error) and even the
illusion of knowledge, do not exist; but, this makes it even
more important that the sense of a new knowledge can and
must descend into the reality of life." (I, 240) In the realm
of images, in which the illogic holds sway, Artaud hoped
to discover new meanings. Any attempt to explain or interpret these images by means of reason could only lead to
their destruction. "Whatever belongs to the realm of the
image cannot be subjected to reason; it must remain within
this realm, or be annihilated." (I, 240)

On the subject of "images" Artaud assumed a far more
extreme position than Breton, asserting that purely verbal
images were not sufficient, and, in fact, were inferior to
plastic or pictorial ones. And where could he better find
these plastic images than in the cinema? In the world of
films he hoped to discover a non-verbal language that could
dispense with logic and reason. His early enthusiasm for the
silent films knew no reservations. Assigning to cinematic
images the same task that the Surrealists had imposed upon
automatic writing, he declared that films must be made to
show the immediate workings of the mind without the intervention of written or spoken words.

Motion pictures are made especially to express mental things —the inner life of consciousness—not so much by the play of images as by something more intangible which restores them to us . . . without intermediaries, or representations. Motion pictures have arrived at a turning point in human thought, at the precise moment when worn-out language is losing its symbolic power, when the mind is weary of the game of representations. (III, 80–81)

Convinced that films should be free of the distortions imposed by rational and logical thought, Artaud wanted the cinema to evoke all that is seemingly dreamlike and unbelievable, but which is essentially more "real" than everyday reality. "Either cinema will come increasingly closer to the realm of fantasy, a realm which, as you will see, is in reality all that which is real, or it will not endure." (III, 81) Coherent plots and logical relationships were to be eschewed; the play of images, forms, and lights in films would suggest actual states of being which were often not subject to rational analysis. Of his own film, *La coquille et le clergyman*, Artaud maintained: "[It] does not tell a story but develops a sequence of mental states, each one derived from the preceding one in the same way that one thought is derived from another without reproducing a reasonable chain of events. True psychic situations stem from the clash of objects and gestures." (III, 76)

While Artaud's theatrical writings have become well known, particularly his *Le théâtre et son double*, not much is known of his contribution to the art of cinema. Yet, many of his ideas on the theater are little more than an extension of what he wrote and said concerning film. A number of his cinematic ideas were influential in the 1920's—a period which saw great activity and experimentation in this medium.[19] In addition, many of Artaud's cinematic theories are relevant to the world of contemporary film. For example, Artaud insisted that objects in films must assume an independent existence, evoking reactions not by what they represent, but by what they are. Objects, he maintained, are more than mere symbols or accessories to the action.

> The smallest details and the most insignificant objects assume their own particular meaning and life. And this is true aside from the value of what the images themselves signify, aside from the thoughts they translate or the symbols which they constitute. By isolating objects, films give them a separate existence which tends more and more to become independent and detached from the ordinary meaning of these objects. (III, 79–80)

How can objects have a "separate existence"? In all likelihood Artaud is referring to Surrealistic films in which objects metamorphose, suddenly grow or diminish, and inexplicably change location without human or mechanical aid. Taking this a step further, it is possible to see how objects in contemporary films can also be said to have an independent existence, although nothing mysterious or inexplicable occurs. In the "new wave" films, the camera focuses upon objects or people, not for their symbolic value or to further plot development (as was the case in the films of the 1930's), but because the object which is thereby singled out for attention evokes a reaction in the audience merely by virtue of its existence.

Another of Artaud's theses (now acquiring a far greater credence than it formerly enjoyed) is that words do not have to be used solely to advance the action depicted in a film. Words, assuming an objectlike existence, can be completely divorced from action. "As far as the talking film is concerned, you will see that this film is talking only to the degree to which the words pronounced are placed there solely to make the image bounce back. Voices are *in space* like objects. And it is on the visual level, so to speak, that they must be accepted." (III, 47) Sounds are important in themselves, and not only as the "physical consequence of a movement or an act." Artaud's objective was to make words play a visual, rather than a verbal, role. Contemporary directors have interpreted this idea each in his own fashion. While sounds are not as yet used to make images "bounce back," the separation of words from images is a frequent device in current films. Godard, in particular, seems to delight in separating words and images—witness such films as *Vivre sa vie, Pierrot le fou,* and *Le petit soldat.*

Artaud and the other Surrealists made the same demands of film that they did of poetry: Both media had to dispense with logical thought and language and reveal, instead, the immediate workings of the mind. Their rejection of rational thought was often accompanied by a willingness to accept mystical and even magical modes of thought in its place. The exact role, however, that the Surrealists accorded to mysticism and occultism is a difficult one to determine; and, consequently, it has given rise to much critical speculation. Maurice Blanchot believes that all the Surrealist techniques, especially hypnotic trances and automatic writing, were used in an attempt to communicate with what he calls the unknown. Corroborating Blanchot's viewpoint, Octavio Paz, the Mexican writer and critic, states that automatic writing can be seen as a modern equivalent of that aspect of Buddhist meditation in which man enters into a passive state inducing perception of true reality.[20]

Similarly, Michel Carrouges, who has devoted an entire book and a long article to an exploration of the influence of occult and esoteric doctrines in Surrealist thought, sees evidence of the mediumistic tradition in automatic writing. For him, automatic writing constitutes a dialogue between

man's rational mind and his unconscious instincts which
secretly communicate with the universe. Carrouges also
deals with other esoteric doctrines, involving evil spirits and
supernatural phenomena, found in Surrealist thought. Lastly,
he draws a parallel between the Surrealistic poetic metaphor
and the process of alchemy, maintaining that Surrealists and
alchemists tried, in their respective ways, to effect a metamorphosis of man and to penetrate the secrets of the universe.[21]

Not all critics, however, share Carrouges' view of Surrealist thought. Ferdinand Alquié, for one, while admitting
that the Surrealist movement was influenced by the occult
tradition, maintains that this tradition was reinterpreted in
psychological terms. Such divergent interpretations of the
importance of mysticism and occultism in Surrealism are partially due to Breton's ambivalent attitude. As Alquié takes
pains to point out, Breton openly rejects mysticism in a number of passages. Declaring that he cannot believe in the
existence of spirits, Breton asserts that true life must be
sought in this world and not elsewhere. Furthermore, this
leader of the Surrealists distinguishes between poetic and
mystical analogies, asserting that the former are empirical
and "do not presuppose an invisible universe beyond the
network of the visible world." Finally, Breton often expresses serious reservations concerning the very principle of
esotericism.[22] Breton was not of one mind however; certain
other of his writings render suspect his explicit denials of
faith in esotericism and mysticism. In his first "Manifesto
of Surrealism," he declares that the Surrealists seek an absolute point in which all contradictions are resolved, a point
where "life and death, the real and the imaginary, the past
and the future, the communicable and the incommunicable,
the high and the low are no longer considered contradictory."[23] Pursuing this same line of thought, Breton later de-

clared that he would accept any philosophy, mystical or not, provided it could reconcile all opposites:

It is well known today that Surrealism would have liked nothing better than to allow the mind to hurdle the barrier raised by contradictions such as action-dream, reason-madness, and sensation-representation. Such contradictions constitute the major obstacle in Occidental thought. In its [Surrealism's] continuous efforts toward this goal, it has always welcomed the support found in Hegel's and Heraclitus' dialectic . . . as well as in the Yin-Yang relationship of Chinese thought, which finds its [logical] conclusion in the philosophy of "Zen."[24]

The concept of such an "absolute point" is not without mystical overtones. In fact, as Carrouges observes, although the idea of a "supreme point" comes from the Cabala, where it is regarded as the moment of creation in which everything existed *ab ovo*, the concept is a fundamental one in all occult doctrines. So, it would seem that there are two André Bretons. While the first denies all belief in occult phenomena, the second is drawn toward mysticism and esotericism.

Although it is difficult to determine to what degree Breton and the other Surrealists actually believed in spiritual phenomena, there can be no question of the influence exerted upon them by mystical and occult thought. And, more than any other member of the group, Artaud came under the sway of occultism. With every year, he grew more and more fascinated by supernatural phenomena until, toward the end of his life, it was impossible to dissuade him from the illusion that he was under the influence of evil spells. Without question, his own problems contributed to his lifelong preoccupation with esoteric and mystical doctrines. In mystical thought the supreme moment arrives when man loses all sense of individual self and becomes one with universal being, or spirit. Liberated from the limitations of body and mind, he is encompassed by a profound sense of peace. This idea of mystical oneness had a special appeal for Artaud because it allowed him legitimately to abandon any attempt at self-control. Artaud–Abelard welcomed Heloise precisely because she took complete charge of him; similarly, Artaud sought peace through mystical moments when he could be rid of all responsibility for his own existence. In one article on Uccello, Artaud makes it clear that he would willingly renounce his existence as an individual. Identifying with a Uccello who has become pure and unlimited consciousness, Artaud–Uccello imagines himself "without any kind of appearance and stripped of any body, just as he would have wanted to be: without any place in space to indicate the location of his mind." (I, 205) Artaud–Uccello has reached an ideal state in which his body has disappeared, and his mind, by uniting with universal consciousness, has ceased to exist in space. Uccello wants to dispense with real lines, in order to paint those which succeed in shedding materiality. "The beautiful myth, the beautiful goal: to paint the disappearance of the form, not the line which encloses all others, but just the one which begins not to exist." (I, 206)

It may seem paradoxical that the Artaud who insisted that all thought and emotion originated in the "marrow of our bones" was also the man who so ardently desired to rid himself of his material being. Throughout his life, Artaud swung from pole to pole. After maintaining that human life could be reduced to physical terms, he would assert that the nature of true existence was spiritual. This contradiction, however, is not difficult to understand: Artaud sought a mystical, non-material realm in which he would be free of his body—free of pain and animal desire. But the very intensity of his desire to escape from corporeality only served to make him more aware than ever of the bondage in which it held him. And so, he would alternate between two opposed positions: either the body was the source of all thought and emotion, or, man had to discard his body and reach a purely spiritual state.

Because mystical union held a promise of peace for Artaud, he was drawn to Oriental religion and philosophy. Well acquainted with Buddhist and Hindu thought, primarily through the works of René Guénon, he had read and reread the sacred books of various Eastern religions, especially the Upanishads, the Tibetan and Egyptian books of the dead, and the Tao Te Ching. In these religions, traditional Western distinctions between knower and known, subject and object, are transcended; everything merges in a higher reality. The Upanishads constantly speak of the transcendent principle called Brahman, or Atman, with which the individual mind must strive to unite. Artaud could not fail to be strongly attracted to this particular concept. Convinced that he had to make his thoughts coincide with his being in order to reach the plenitude of existence he so desired, he welcomed a philosophy preaching the indissolubility of thought and being. But this was not the only aspect of Hindu thought which appealed to him; he also found comfort in the relatively unimportant role that Hindu philosophers ascribe to rational thought. Hindu thinkers believe that true reality is spiritual in nature and can be perceived intuitively without the aid of the rational mind.

> This insistence upon immediate perception rather than on abstract reasoning is what distinguishes the Indian philosophy of religion from philosophy as Western nations know it. Immediate perception is the source from which springs all Indian thought.
>
> This perception, it must be made clear, is not of the senses, nor must it be confused with the operations of the intellect, nor of the emotions; it is supersensuous, transcen-

dental—something not to be fully explained in rational terms.[25]

Artaud was drawn to mysticism and to Surrealism by the characteristic the two had in common: The subsidiary role accorded rational thought in Eastern religion coincides perfectly with the Surrealists' rejection of Western logic and reason. Surrealism could even be called "mystical" insofar as it insists that true reality cannot be perceived by the logical mind.

The mark of Eastern mysticism is particularly evident in the articles Artaud published anonymously in *la Révolution surréaliste*. In *"A Table"* ("Come and Dine") Artaud exhorts men to rid themselves of logical thought and join with the transcendent spirit in a moment of spiritual union. "Come forth from the caves of being. Come. Spirit breathes beyond spirit. It is time to abandon your dwellings. Yield to Omniscient-Thought." (I, 252) Here Artaud is giving voice to the Hindu belief that man can achieve supreme spiritual union only if he is able to escape from his physical being. Addressing the Dalai Lama, Artaud pleads:

> Show us, Lama, the material levitation of bodies and how we might no longer be held by the earth.
> For, you know full well to what transparent liberation of souls, to what liberty of Spirit in Spirit, we refer, O acceptable Pope, O Pope in the true Spirit. (I, 262)

Many of the poems Artaud wrote in the 1920's also reflect ardent mystical desires. One such poem, *"Extase"* ("Ecstasy"), voices his wish to transcend his individual being and to unite with transcendent principles.

> Exhausting quest of the self
> Penetration which transcends itself
> Ah! to join the log of ice

With the mind that conceived it.

(I, 191)

Images conjured up with phrases such as a "log of ice," referring to objects which do not exist in the normal world, are often used in mystical literature to express the ineffable. Artaud may hope that by joining his mind to the ineffable, he can soar beyond himself. It is also possible that he wants to effect a fusion between his mind and whatever it may be concerned with, at any particular moment, in order to insure that his "empty" mind will never lack for content. In a moment of "ecstasy" his mind and its thoughts would be fused into an indissoluble unity.

"Prière" ("Prayer"), another early poem, expresses once again Artaud's desire to attain a transcendent realm:

> Untie us. Sever us
> With your hands of cutting embers
> Open up these burning roads
> Where one dies beyond death
>
> Make our brains reel
> In the bosom of their own knowledge
> And ravish us of our intelligence
> With the claws of a new typhoon.

(I, 350)

Here again, Artaud employs the terminology of mysticism ("burning roads") to describe the desired ineffable state. Hoping for release from all that is earthy and material, he longs to be reborn in a spiritual world "where one dies beyond death." To reach this, he must renounce his intellect ("And ravish us of our intelligence")—something he would do most willingly. The ease with which Artaud surrenders his intelligence recalls his attitude with the clairvoyant: he is glad to rid himself of his intellect, and, consequently, of any responsibility for his own being. Justifying his attitude, Ar-

taud declares that by suppressing his rational mind he is able
to enjoy the illusion of establishing contact with hidden
forces, an illusion which seems more real than reality. "I
close the eyes of my intelligence, and, by letting the unformu-
lated speak within me, I give myself the illusion of a system
whose terms escape me. But this moment of error gives me
the feeling that I have ravished something real from the
unknown." (I, 106)

Many of Artaud's reflections on death are also bathed in
a hazy mysticism. He had read the Egyptian and Tibetan
books of the dead which describe the journey taken by a
man's soul after death. These books, like the Greek philosophical systems of Neo-Pythagoreanism and Orphism, maintain that the soul can be reborn only after it is freed from
the body—its earthly embodiment which is unclean and con-
temptible. Artaud, who was conversant with this philosophical concept, expresses precisely this idea in asserting that
death allows us to "empty existence, on the one hand, and,
on the other, to regain the emptiness of a crystalline liberty."
(I, 279) And in a letter to a clairvoyant, Artaud makes it
clear that he experiences a sensation of peace and calm from
the knowledge that his death is near. "Before my death, I was
aware that it completed a life which had finally become calm
and sweeter than my best memories." (I, 125) The knowledge
of approaching death makes it possible for Artaud to cope
with life; death sheds a "perfect and sweet light where our
souls no longer make us suffer, although they are still in-
fested with evil. A light which reveals without cruelty or
passion one single atmosphere, the atmosphere of a pious,
serene and precious fatalism." (I, 124) Death, and the fatalism it implies, attracts Artaud because with it comes the cer-
tainty that, since all is controlled by destiny, his futile attempts to direct his being will no longer be necessary.

Orphic theology viewed the world as a divine unity to

which the soul returned after death, and regarded the names
of gods as "nothing more than the different terms for the
manifold effects and manifestations of the One divine Being which formed the kernel of the whole world."[26] This
same idea is clearly presented by Artaud in his own description of the journey taken by the souls of the dead. He calls
such souls "intelligences."

> By investigating death, we would perceive the Secret of the
> divine ascendancy and of the spiritual configuration of the
> world . . . It is in fact highly unlikely that these intelli-
> gences, after they are purified by casting off their corporeal
> shell and re-enter the great spiritual all . . . will be incapa-
> ble of penetrating the secret of the origin and destiny of
> things. (I, 168)

Thus death will enable the soul to make contact with spiritual realities and to comprehend the true nature of the
cosmos.

Artaud's eagerness to learn the secrets that only death can
reveal led him to suggest that we should attempt to approxi-
mate a deathlike state by disrupting our normal psychic
condition.

> I assert . . . that death is not outside the realm of the mind,
> and that within certain limits it is knowable and can be
> approached by a certain mental sensibility. Everything in
> the category of written things which abandons the domain
> of clear and ordered perception, everything which aims to
> create an upheaval of appearances, and to introduce doubts
> concerning the relationship of mental images to each other
> . . . offers a path to death and puts us into contact with
> purer mental states in whose bosoms death is expressed.[27]

The influence of Surrealism, as well as of mysticism, is clearly
discernible in this passage. The call for the disruption of

our normal modes of perception and for the abandonment of logical thought echoes Breton's ringing manifestoes. The same personal problems which led Artaud to embrace certain aspects of Surrealism and mysticism were soon to lead him even farther afield—to the theater of the Orient and to the pagan culture of ancient Mexico.

III

MYTH
AND
MAGIC

At first glance, what Artaud wrote in the 1930's appears to mark a radical departure from his earlier work. No direct mention of his own problems is found in the major works of this period: *Le théâtre et son double, Le moine, Héliogabale, Les nouvelles révélations de l'être,* and *D'un voyage au pays des Tarahumaras.* However, many of the themes which dominate his earlier writings are also found in these books, albeit in veiled form. Although Artaud no longer speaks in subjective terms, it soon becomes clear that he remains obsessed with sexuality and fearful of his own subconscious instincts, while his rejection of normal discursive language and his dislike of Western society, with its traditional faith in the power of logic and rationality, have grown stronger than ever. For the first time though—and this is what distinguishes these writings from the earlier ones—Artaud's fears and desires are expressed in universal terms. In an attempt to transcend, or perhaps to justify, his own problems, Artaud seeks to demonstrate that those fears and desires haunt all of Western civilization. And, contemporary culture, or at least segments thereof, does indeed reflect various aspects of Artaud's problems. But no one has suffered from these problems as intensely as Artaud himself.

The element most characteristic of Artaud's work during the 30's is violence, a violence often bringing in its wake perverted sexuality. Artaud's fascination with the more savage aspects of human life no doubt stems, in part, from his experience with the Surrealists. Surrealist movies (*Un chien andalou,* for example) and Surrealist painters (de Chirico and Dali, to name but two) reveal that the Surrealist universe is menaced by inexplicable, malevolent forces of destruction. The Surrealists made no secret of their admiration for the eighteenth-century exponent of sadism and perversion, the Marquis de Sade. On the surface their infatuation with the "divine marquis" appears to contradict their exaltation of the beneficial powers of physical love. This seemingly fundamental ambiguity is open to a number of possible explanations. They may have hoped that the sight of brutality and savage eroticism would encourage man to unleash his own repressed instincts and thus recover his buried psychic energy. Perhaps too, as Ferdinand Alquié suggests, the Surrealists, like Sade and Lautréamont before them, praised fiendish and bloodthirsty acts as a form of rebellion against the human condition.[1] Artaud, more than any other member of the Surrealist group, plunged wholly into the world of violence; the erotic and demonic elements he found in Surrealism only reinforced his own basic tendencies.

In his first work of this period, *Le théâtre et son double,* Artaud pronounces the theater to be the medium par excellence for violence and cruelty; and the essay "Le théâtre et la peste" ("The Theater and the Plague") draws a parallel between the action of the theater and that of the plague. It is Artaud's thesis, presented with arguments distinguished by poetic brilliance rather than logic, that the theater and the plague are alike in that the violence each inspires is capable of liberating man's innermost forces. Reduced to these simple terms, the argument sounds absurd, but Artaud develops his theory with a force and sincerity such as to lure the reader into agreement. Comparing the theater to the plague, Artaud explains:

> If the core of the theater is like the plague, it is not because it is contagious, but because, like the plague, it is the revelation, the bringing forth, the exteriorization of a substratum of latent cruelty by means of which all the depraved possibilities of the mind converge in an individual or a people. (IV, 37)

Artaud's fear of his uncontrollable subconscious instincts has already been noted. He welcomes the advent of the plague precisely because it unleashes these instincts—which he now calls evil—in all men. "Like the plague the theater is the time of evil, the triumph of somber forces that are nourished by an even deeper force until their extinction." (IV, 37) His conviction that our repressed instincts are perverted and evil leaves no room for even a fleeting notion that some goodness may lurk in the recesses of man's being. He believes that our dreams disclose the terror and cruelty which govern our fundamental instincts. And it is the task of the theater to present these dreams in all their nightmarish reality.

> The public will believe in the theater's dreams only if it can see them as true dreams and not as a servile copy of reality, and only if they [the dreams] allow the public to liberate within itself the magical liberty of dreams which are only recognizable [as such] when they are imprinted with terror and cruelty. (IV, 103)

A few pages farther on Artaud tells us that dreams reveal man's "taste for crime, his erotic obsessions, his savagery." It is interesting to compare the most famous modern description of the plague, that by Albert Camus, with Artaud's. For Camus, the plague—a symbol of all unforeseen, inexplicable disasters—brings out the goodness in man by making him aware of the necessity to help his fellow man in a common struggle against the forces of evil. For Artaud, on the other hand, the plague releases man's worst, most violent, instincts. Where Camus is clinical, Artaud delights in gory descriptions of what occurs when plague strikes.

> The streets are already congested by the dead heaped up in crumbling pyramids whose edges are gnawed by animals. The flamelike stink rises in the air. Entire streets are blocked by the piles of the dead. Then houses open and delirious victims, whose minds are full of frightful images, spread howling through the streets . . . Over the bloody, thick, poisonous streams, colored like agony and opium, which gush out of the corpses, strange characters pass, dressed in wax with noses like Pinocchio's and glass eyes . . . chanting absurd litanies whose power cannot keep them from sinking into the fire in their turn. (IV, 29)

Artaud wants to project man's violent instincts—lust, vengeance, the drive for power—onto the stage where they will be transformed into symbols. "[The theater] revives all our dormant conflicts and all their powers, and gives these powers names which we hail as symbols." (IV, 34) His ideal theater would thus resemble primitive rites in which different members of the community played the roles of Death, Lust, Hate, etc. In this manner the theater allows man to portray instincts capable of destroying society if released in the world of reality. "These symbols . . . burst forth in the guise of incredible images which give full rights and existence to acts that are by nature hostile to the life of societies." (IV, 34) In other words, Artaud justifies his conception of the theater with the argument of theatrical catharsis: man

can rid himself of undesirable desires and drives by presenting them on stage.

Since, however, this idea of catharsis rests on a somewhat
shaky premise, Artaud's critics have not been slow to pose
disturbing questions. Paul Arnold, for example, asks if it is
possible to assume that a liberation of evil forces would lead
to good. History, he says, indicates that once man's thirst
for violence is aroused, the only result is still greater violence. And, he adds, "Any true mystic, any authentic yogi
will teach us that the release of evil is different from the
release of good and that the latter cannot be nourished by
the former even if evil disappears in the process."[2] Other
critics have been more severe regarding this phase of Artaud's theatrical writings. Alan Seymour, for instance, sees
analogies between Artaud's concept of cruelty and certain
aspects of the Hitlerian regime.[3]

Any mention of violence in Artaud's work is inevitably
accompanied by another word—cruelty. It was not by accident that the theatrical group he established in 1934 was
called the "Theater of Cruelty." Afraid lest his readers
equate cruelty with physical violence, Artaud sought to make
it clear that the cruelty he had in mind was not brutal and
sadistic but cosmic and metaphysical. The task of the theater,
he maintained, is to show that life itself is cruel because
metaphysical forces are constantly at work to deprive man
of his freedom. It appears more than likely that Artaud's
concern with man's lack of free will stems from his inability
to direct his own life. It is as if he wants to reassure himself that he is not the only one to have been determined
by forces beyond his control.

> As soon as I have said "cruelty" everyone will jump to
> the conclusion that it means "blood." But a "theater of
> cruelty" means a theater which is difficult and cruel for my-
> self first of all. . . . it does not mean the cruelty we can

exercise upon each other by cutting up each others' bodies, and sawing up our personal anatomies, or, like Assyrian emperors, sending bags of human ears, noses, or neatly carved-off nostrils through the mail, but the much more dreadful and necessary cruelty which things can exercise against us. We are not free. The sky can still fall on our heads. And the theater has been made to teach us that first of all. (IV, 95)

Artaud's belief that life is cruel also seems related to his own problems, for whenever he attempts to prove or justify that belief, the reasons he advances are less than convincing. On a few occasions, he hints at the personal connotations that the word "cruelty" has for him. In one such passage, he introduces a key word, "evil." "In the flame of life, in the appetite for life, in the irrational impulsion to live, there is a kind of initial malice. . . . In the manifested world, metaphysically speaking, evil is the permanent law." (IV, 123–124) Artaud's use of the word "evil" is revealing; while life can conceivably be called "cruel," it cannot be said to be "evil." Evil is a concept which belongs to an entirely different realm—the realm of morality and religion wherein reside absolute good and absolute bad. The notion of evil can play no role in a world of impersonal metaphysical forces. But since Artaud appears to use "cruel" and "evil" interchangeably, the question is not why Artaud considers life to be cruel, but why he thinks it is evil. The preceding chapter pointed out Artaud's attraction to religious systems such as Orphism, Gnosticism, and Neo-Pythagoreanism—systems which hold the immortal soul to be imprisoned in a world of matter exemplified by man's unclean and corrupt body. Distinct gnostic leanings can be detected in Artaud's statement that "metaphysically speaking, because life involves extension, thickness, heaviness, and matter, it involves, as a direct consequence, evil and all that is inherent in evil, space, extension and matter." (IV, 137) Artaud obviously believes that life is evil (or cruel) because it cannot escape from matter. Conversely, he praises the theater for its capacity to release us from the inertia of matter weighing us down; the theater impels men "to see themselves as they are, it makes the mask fall, it uncovers lies, flabbiness, baseness and hypocrisy; it shakes off the asphyxiating inertia of matter." (IV, 39) Upon examination, Artaud's grand notion of cruelty is based on slender philosophical ground: life can be called cruel only if we assume that matter is basically evil. Such an assumption raises fundamental problems, many of which have been astutely analyzed by Nicola Chiaromonte, who observes:

> As a matter of fact, we are in the midst of what I shall call, for lack of a more precise term, Artaud's "gnosticism"—his bottomless pessimism about the nature of the real world and his hatred of it, as a place of shadows and evil, which can be redeemed only by the effort of creation, the act of incarnating and personifying physically, for creation is a drive toward the light and the good. But it can never redeem completely. For in order to incarnate and personify, the creative principle must accept matter, which is the principle of evil, and the form of the world as it is.[4]

In other words, creation aims for the light, seeking to abolish corrupt matter; at the same time, however, it depends upon matter for its existence. A logical impasse is thus created: By destroying matter, creation would only destroy itself.

The fundamental ambiguity characterizing Artaud's concept of cruelty was also evident whenever he proposed ways of presenting violence and cruelty on stage. While he continually asserted that the cruelty he envisioned was cosmic and was not to be equated with physical violence, all the plays he suggested producing were permeated by blood and gore. He hoped, for example, that the Theater of Cruelty would stage Elizabethan melodramas, a tale by the Marquis de Sade, the story of Bluebeard, and Büchner's *Wozzeck*—all of which contain elements of sadism and horror. It is possible to defend Artaud's choice of plays by pointing out the difficulty of illustrating metaphysical cruelty, and the dearth of better examples. However, it seems far more likely that Artaud tried to justify his innate attraction to sadism and violence by raising violence and cruelty to a universal, metaphysical level.

This attempt at justification is well illustrated in *Les Cenci*, the only play Artaud completed. The play deals with a Renaissance nobleman, a monster named Cenci who rapes his daughter and is killed, in turn, by assassins she has hired. Far from regretting his vicious nature, Cenci glories in the evil deeds he has committed. "I am no longer concerned with anything but refining my crimes. A beautiful, black master-piece is the only heritage that I care about leaving." (IV, 190) Artaud tries to infuse a feeling of cosmic cruelty into the play by having Cenci represent the evil forces of nature, not unlike the plague. The rapist declares:

> More than once it has happened that I have identified with destiny in a dream. This explains my vices and my natural inclination toward hatred. . . . I consider myself, and in fact I am, a force of nature. For me, there is neither life, nor death, nor god, nor incest, nor repentance, nor crime. . . .
>
> I seek and do evil by intention and principle. I am un-able to resist the forces which burn to stampede within me. (IV, 191)

Speeches such as this, however, pale alongside scenes of mur-der, rape, and torture.

Artaud planned writing another play, *La conquête du Mexique (The Conquest of Mexico)*—also to be produced by the Theater of Cruelty. In this, he intended to deal with

the bloody struggle for power between the Mexican Indians
and their ruthless Spanish conquerors. The finished outline
of this play expresses Artaud's desire to present man as the
pawn of historical and metaphysical forces. Despite these
lofty aims, it is clear from the outline that a dominant role
in the play was to be assigned to bloodshed and physical violence. Curiously enough, Artaud portrays the bloody battle
between the Indians and the Spaniards in much the same
lyrical way that he describes the plague in *Le théâtre et son
double*.

> A religious fervor causes heads to bow. . . . These are the
> funeral rites of Montezuma. A stamping, a murmur. The
> crowd of natives whose steps sound like the jaws of a scorpion.
> Then stirrings in front of the miasmas, enormous heads
> with noses swollen with the stink—and nothing but Span-
> iards who are immense but on crutches. And like a tidal
> wave, like the sharp burst of a storm, like rain whipping on
> the sea, the revolt carries off the whole crowd in groups,
> with the body of the dead Montezuma tossing on their heads
> like a ship. And the sharp spasms of the battle, the foam of
> the heads of the cornered Spaniards who are squashed like
> blood against the ramparts that are turning green. (V, 28–29)

The sexual perversions found in *Les Cenci* occur, in one
form or another, in virtually everything Artaud wrote during the 1930's. In his description of the plague, for example,
Artaud does not fail to mention that the disease heightens
eroticism, adding that many recovered victims, instead of
fleeing the city, attempt to find pleasure with the dying, or
even with the dead. At one point in *Le théâtre et son double* he implies that all our violent instincts are sexual in
nature. Although he does not fully understand the link between sexuality on the one hand and violence and evil on
the other, Artaud is convinced that such a link exists. "We
can now say that all true freedom is sinister, and merges

infallibly with sexual freedom which is also sinister, although we do not know precisely why." (IV, 37) The libido, which Artaud equates with sexuality, is made to appear ugly and repulsive. "For it has been a long time since the Platonic Eros, the procreative sense, the freedom of life, vanished beneath the gloomy coating of the *Libido* which can be identified with all that is dirty, abject and ignominious in the act of living." (IV, 37–38) Since Artaud believes that matter and the body are evil, it follows naturally that he should consider sexuality sordid and ugly and that he should label our bodily functions "abject" and "dirty." Just as the word "evil" seems inappropriate, so, too, do the words "abject" and "dirty" seem misplaced here. Like "evil," these words imply that an ideal realm of goodness, or, in this case, purity, exists. Such a concept has religious, and more especially, Christian, overtones. Yet Artaud himself would be the first to deny any belief in Christianity. Once again, it appears that the intensity of his personal problems was such that he was forced to embrace attitudes and ideas that he could not logically defend.

One form of perverted sexuality which particularly interested Artaud was incest. *Les Cenci,* as has been noted, narrates the story of a man who rapes his daughter and is then assassinated by her hirelings. One of the essays in *Le théâtre et son double,* titled *"La mise en scène et la métaphysique"* ("Stage Sets and Metaphysics"), describes a painting which, says the author, presents metaphysical realities. The canvas, by Lucas van Leyden, depicts the Biblical character Lot watching his daughters "parade up and down as if he were a guest at a prostitutes' banquet." (IV, 41) Concludes Artaud: "We are thus presented with the deeply incestuous nature of the old theme which the painter develops here in passionate images." (IV, 41)

Incest plays an important role also in *Le moine,* Artaud's

adaptation of Lewis' gothic novel *The Monk*. Summarized briefly, *Le moine* is the story of a Spanish monk, Ambrosio, who falls in love with Antonia, a beautiful and innocent young girl. Aided by a voluptuous seductress, who is in reality an evil spirit in league with the devil, Ambrosio kills Antonia's mother and carries off her daughter to underground tombs. There he rapes and kills her. At the book's conclusion, as Ambrosio is about to die a justly horrible death, he learns that he was Antonia's brother and that the two women he killed were his mother and sister. The plot is further complicated by the presence of a fanatic Mother Superior who inflicts unspeakable tortures on one of the young nuns, Agnes, when the latter discloses that she is pregnant. Detailed descriptions of brutality and torture abound in the novel. When Agnes, for example, is buried alive in a tomb inhabited by skeletons and worms, she refuses to relinquish the rotting corpse of her dead infant. The theme of the hermaphrodite (which will be fully developed in *Héliogabale*) is also touched upon in *Le moine*. The evil temptress responsible for leading Ambrosio astray by awakening his sexual desires, first appears to him dressed as a young boy. Although from a moral viewpoint, Ambrosio is as different from Abelard as one could imagine, it is nevertheless interesting that both are destroyed by the forces of sex. Artaud obviously wants to prove that sex is undeniably evil.

Similar passages devoted to cruelty and sexual violence constitute a considerable portion of *Héliogabale*, a poetic biography of the emperor Heliogabalus, who ruled Rome from 218 to 222. Although Artaud was asked to write this book by his publishers, there is no question but that he was attracted to the title character because of the sadism and violence traditionally associated with the latter's reign. Consistently choosing to emphasize these elements, Artaud dwells on Heliogabalus' flagrant homosexuality, and is at pains to point out that the emperor was descended from a line of virile women and received his unbringing from a eunuch, whom he later murdered. A curious reversal of the conventional sexual roles occurs in *Héliogabale* in which weak, emasculated men are manipulated by dominating women. Artaud, further, does not permit us to forget that Heliogabalus' mother, whose father had committed parricide, was little more than a prostitute and that she shared an incestuous love with her son. Sexual excesses, as well as scenes of senseless brutality, are scattered throughout the book. Vivid tableaux of enforced castrations which occurred under Heliogabalus' rule, and of the violent manner of his death, haunt the reader.

Artaud found it no more difficult to identify with the violent Heliogabalus than with the innocuous figures of Abelard and Uccello. A letter to Jean Paulhan informs us that Artaud felt he had described himself in the person of the emperor. And Anaïs Nin recounts, in fictionalized form, a visit she made to the Louvre with Artaud, whom she calls "Pierre." Leading her to a statue of Heliogabalus, Pierre asked if she saw any resemblance between the Roman emperor and himself. Miss Nin, apparently, answered in the affirmative.

> In the face of stone I saw the face of Pierre. I saw the face of Pierre when he returned behind life, behind the flesh word, into the mineral, everything drawn inward and petrified. I saw the face of Pierre in which nothing moved except the eyes, and the eyes moved like a terrified ocean, seeking wildly to withdraw also, but unable to, still liquid, still foaming and smoking, and this effort of the water in his body against the invasion and petrification of the stone, made the bitter sweat break out all over his body.[5]

The kinship Artaud sensed with the decadent, homosexual Roman emperor reflects the doubts he experienced regarding his own virility. Conversely, his admiration for Heliogabalus stems from a belief that the emperor had succeeded in reconciling the male and female elements within himself. In an attempt to convince us of this, Artaud offers several different arguments but, as is so often the case, his reasons are poetic rather than logical. He asserts that Heliogabalus was able to reconcile the sexual principles within himself because, although effeminate, he was the high priest of a phallic cult which worshiped the sun as the source of the Masculine Principle. "Heliogabalus, the homosexual king who wants to be a woman, is a priest of the Masculine. He realizes within himself the identity of opposites but he does not realize it without difficulty; his religious homosexuality is caused by nothing other than a determined and abstract struggle between the Masculine and the Feminine." (VII, 74) Heliogabalus had brought this cult to Rome from ancient Syria. According to Artaud, the fact that the high priest of this cult incarnated the conflicting sexual principles in his own person reflected the Syrians' desire to see these opposing principles reconciled. Toward this end, they dedicated temples to the sun and the moon, to the phallus and the vagina. "Heliogabalus is man and woman. And the religion of the sun is the religion of man, but he cannot do anything without woman, his double, wherein he is reflected." (VII, 103) Artaud interprets Heliogabalus' every act as an attempt to reconcile the opposing poles of masculinity and femininity; he even asserts that the emperor castrated men in an effort to unify the conflicting sexual principles within them. Thus, indirectly, does Artaud reveal his own passionate desire to unite the male and female within him and thereby eliminate his inner sexual conflict.

Héliogabale is not Artaud's only work to present this male-female dichotomy. In fact, most of the books Artaud wrote during the 1930's reflect his ever-growing fascination with primitive religions whose cosmologies explain the world's genesis in terms of masculine and feminine principles. Artaud expounds upon the fact that primitive societies have always been violently torn by the struggle between the two sexual principles. He apparently hopes to prove that violence has always been the handmaiden of sex. One passage in *Le théâtre et son double* affirms that the important myths of mankind all speak of the moment when the sexual principles were violently torn asunder. "And that is why all the great Myths are somber, and why all the magnificent Fables, which tell the crowds of the first sexual division and of the first slaughter of essences which appeared in creation, can only be imagined in an atmosphere of slaughter, torture and bloodshed." (IV, 38)

Artaud dedicated *Héliogabale* to the twin forces of anarchy and sex; it is precisely these forces that drew him to the Tarahumara civilization which he later described in *D'un voyage au pays des Tarahumaras*. His contact with the Tarahumara culture brought home to him that the ancient Syrians were not the only ones to have reconciled the opposing sexual principles; he became convinced that the Male and Female principles existed simultaneously within the Tarahumara race. As proof of this, he offered his discovery that the Indians' ritual dances often involved the peyote plant, whose very form symbolizes the reconciliation of the sexual principles. "At the feet of each sorcerer is *one* hole at whose bottom the Male and Female of Nature, represented by the hermaphroditic roots of the peyote plant (we know that the peyote plant assumes the form of the intertwined sexes of a man and a woman), sleep in Matter, that is, in the Concrete." (T, 75) The Tarahumara dances also revealed the underlying conflict of these forces. Artaud gives us his own interpretation of one such dance:

It was no longer a man and a woman who were there, but two principles: the male, open-mouthed, with chattering, red, inflamed, bloody gums which looked as if they had been slashed by the roots of his teeth which were translucent just then, like commanding tongues; the female, a toothless ghost, with molars full of holes which had been filled, like a rat in a trap, frustrated in her heat, fleeing and turning in front of the hairy male. They were going to collide with each other, to plunge themselves into each other with frenzy . . . finally intertwining in front of the *indiscreet* and *guilty* eyes of God, who would be replaced, little by little, by their action. (T, 24–25)

The woman's bestial desires reduce her to a repulsive rat in heat while the man, although virile and born to command, is almost as ugly as she. The sexual act "replaces" God insofar as human beings, by mating and producing offspring, play a role analogous to that of God-the-creator. A few lines farther on, Artaud attempts to disassociate the idea of sex, which he abhors, from that of God. In order to do so, he views sex as the emanation of a sort of universal subconscious. "For I believed I saw in this Dance the point where the universal subconscious is sick. And it is quite apart from God." (T, 26) The subject of sexuality leads Artaud back to the question of evil. This time, however, his statements are far less ambiguous than in *Le théâtre et son double*, for he admits that the opposite of "evil" is not "good," but rather, "purity." "Evil is in all things and I myself, as a man, can no longer feel that I am pure. Something dreadful rises up within me; it does not come from me but from the darkness that I have within me, from that part of me where man's soul does not know where the Self begins and where it ends." (T, 29) The implication here is that man's hidden, evil forces stem from mysterious (or subconscious) instincts within him.

And, without doubt, the most terrifying of all these instincts is sexuality.

Artaud's obsessive fear of woman and of sexuality is best seen in *Les nouvelles révélations de l'être*, the last work of this period. Convinced that the natural forces of the universe have been disturbed by women, Artaud insists that a day will come when man will once again dominate. "In a world delivered over to woman's sexuality, the spirit of man is going to regain its rights." (VII, 156) When this new age dawns, not only will the sexes be separated, but love itself will be banished from the earth. An "initiation" will make certain that everything pertaining to sexuality will be burned so that the "Supremacy of Man" can finally be established.

It is true that Artaud was drawn to pagan religions because their myths and rituals expressed the twin forces of anarchy and sex which, he said, had been repressed in modern civilization. But other factors also account for his interest in primitive societies. During the 1920's Artaud had turned his back on Western logic and rationality in favor of Oriental mysticism. His praise of the primitive Tarahumara culture is an extension of his earlier rejection of Western civilization. In this respect, Artaud reflected an attitude common to most of the Surrealists. André Breton himself found close affinities between Surrealist thought and so-called "primitive" thought in that both sought to "suppress the hegemony of consciousness . . . in order to concentrate on the conquest of revelatory emotions."[6] Breton was convinced that contemporary society could be revitalized through an examination of the myths of primitive people. But how could modern man—who had lost all communion with nature and all sense of inner unity—become receptive to these ancient animistic myths? For Breton, the answer lay in poetry. He believed that poetry—which he considered man's original language—could allow us to escape from the destructive bonds of logic and rationality. By rendering man aware of his innermost needs and emotions, poetry could permit him to recover "the primordial feeling that he has about himself, [a feeling] which has been corrupted by positivist rationalism."[7] Once revived by poetry, the ancient myths will effect a metamorphosis of man so that human nature will flourish once again in an uncorrupted state. At the heart of Breton's statements is the belief that poetry and myth are capable of re-establishing man's former communion with the forces of nature. For, unlike Camus and other contemporary thinkers, the Surrealists rejected the idea that nature is indifferent to man. On the contrary, as Breton declared:

> They [the Surrealists] arc very far from admitting that nature is hostile to man, and allege [instead] that man has lost certain keys which he formerly possessed—keys which kept him in close communion with nature. Since then, he has persisted, ever more feverishly, in trying other keys which don't work.
>
> Scientific knowledge of nature will only be worth something if contact with nature can be re-established by poetic, and, if I dare say so, by mythical means.[8]

Breton's belief that poetry possesses the power to uncover cosmic secrets has definite affinities with magical modes of thought. In fact, Octavio Paz uses the word "magical" to describe Breton's conviction that poetry can change the nature of man and reality.[9] In this respect, the Surrealists were worthy descendants of nineteenth-century poets such as Hugo, Nerval, Rimbaud and Baudelaire, who believed that they had been assigned a sacred mission to uncover metaphysical realities hidden to less gifted mortals.

Many of Breton's ideas on animistic religions, poetry, and myth find warm support in Artaud's work. It should be noted that contemporary linguists and anthropologists would take both Artaud and Breton to task for many of their ideas regarding primitive cultures and poetic language. Claude Lévi-Strauss, for example, would take violent exception to their assertion that poetry and myth are closely related. The French anthropologist believes the contrary to be true: ·

> Myth is the part of language where the formula traddut-tore, tradittore reaches its lowest truth value. From that point of view it should be placed in the gamut of linguistic expressions at the end opposite to that of poetry, in spite of all the claims which have been made to prove the contrary.
>
> Poetry is a kind of speech which cannot be translated except at the cost of previous distortions; whereas the mythical value of the myth is preserved through the worst translation.[10]

Regrettably, this work cannot even begin to investigate the linguistic or anthropological accuracy of Artaud's theories, for that would lead far afield. We can only hope to show that Artaud's ideas concerning primitive cultures and myth are closely related to the body of his work, and that they reflect his own problems and preoccupations.

The term "culture" has been used frequently in the preceding paragraphs. Actually, the word had a particular significance for Artaud. Careful to distinguish between culture and civilization, Artaud repeatedly declared that a culture embodied man's metaphysical outlook, while a civilization was nothing more than the body of arbitrary forms assumed by social institutions.[11] He also protested the use of the word "culture" in referring to the arts, maintaining that true culture could not be equated with the art forms of a civilization unless those forms were intimately related to its spiritual, or religious, life. Comparing Occidental to Oriental culture, Artaud decries the fact that European man has reduced culture to the level of an esthetic game unrelated to man's basic needs and desires. Artaud refuses to separate culture from life, "as if there were culture on the one hand and life on the other, as if true culture were not a refined means of understanding and *exercising* life." (IV, 14) European society has grown decadent precisely because culture has been excluded from everyday life. True culture, for Artaud, was still to be found in Mexico, where art plays a religious, or magical, role in the life of the people. In Mexico, art does not exist merely for men to *look* at.

> To our disinterested and inert idea of art an authentic culture opposes a magical and violently egotistical, i.e., involved, idea. The Mexicans capture the *Manas,* the forces latent in every form, which cannot be released by a contemplation of these forms for themselves, but which spring forth from a magical identification with these forms. And the old Totems are there to hasten the communication. (IV, 16)

Understandably, Greek drama, as well as Mexican art, attracted Artaud, for art also played an important spiritual role in ancient Greece. Although Artaud might have denied it, his concept of culture was essentially religious, insofar as he maintained that true culture must reveal to man metaphysical realities and spiritual truths.

Artaud blamed the decadence in European culture on the fact that it had fallen under the influence of intellectual and logical systems of thought. Reaffirming his rejection of logical thought, he asserted that philosophical systems could never affect the vital part of man's life. So-called "civilized" man has, in effect, lost touch with the actual forces of life. "A civilized man is judged by his behavior and he thinks the same way he behaves, but the very word 'civilized' invites confusion: everyone thinks that a cultivated, civilized man is one who knows about systems, and who thinks in systems, forms, signs, and representations." (IV, 12–13)

In a series of lectures delivered at the University of Mexico, Artaud demanded that we return to the beliefs and myths of primitive man who was not "corrupted" by civilization. Like Rousseau, Artaud attributes a mythical past to humanity; he asks for a "cultural revolution," a return to the "great epochs" of history when man was still in touch with the forces of nature. "Beneath the contributions of modern science which disclose [new] forces day after day, there are other unknown and subtle forces, which are not yet part of the scientific domain, but which can become part of it one day. These forces form part of the animated domain of nature known to men during pagan times." (M, 70–71)

Artaud was consistently attracted to what Ernst Cassirer has termed the "mythical thinking" inherent in primitive cultures. Abstract ideas are utterly foreign to mythical thought which, for example, fails to distinguish between an object, which is concrete, and its name, which is abstract. Hence, primitive peoples believed that if magic spells were cast upon a man's name, the man himself would come to harm. The name did more than simply represent the man. "Where we see mere representation, myth, insofar as it has not deviated from its fundamental and original form, sees real identity. The image does not represent the thing; it *is* the thing."[12] Because of an inability to distinguish between the abstract and the concrete, mythical thinking places matter and the mind, or physical and psychic phenomena, in the same category. Consequently, it confuses matter and its attributes, whether those attributes are immaterial forces or material substances. As an illustration of this confusion, Cassirer calls to our attention various myths of creation which explain how the world evolved from a single material substance which divided itself into other substances and into nonmaterial forces. And even these forces were assigned a material base. "Mythical thinking answers the questions of origins by reducing even intricate complexes of relations . . . to a pre-existing material substance. And because of this fundamental form of thought, all mere properties or attributes must for myth ultimately become bodies."[13]

Mythical thinking doesn't merely confuse the abstract and the concrete, but also establishes connections between all things, with the result that any similarity is seen "as an indication of an original kinship, an essential identity." Space, time, and number are all interconnected for the following reason: Because primitive peoples constantly distinguished between the sacred and the profane, all objects, and actions, were either worshiped or feared. The quality of sacredness was transferred from particular persons or things to their spatial or temporal determinations, thereby rendering places and numbers sacred. For example, the number four was holy because it expressed the cardinal points of the universe.

> All existence is articulated in the form of space and all change in the rhythm and periodicity of time, every attribute which adheres to a specific spatial-temporal *place,* is immediately transferred to the *content* that is given it; while conversely, the special character of the content gives a distinguishing character to the place in which it is situated.[14]

Aware of the interrelationship of everything in the universe, primitive man saw himself as an integral part of nature. Through his rites and rituals he sought to communicate with cosmic rhythms and to learn the secrets of life and death. His desire to achieve oneness with the whole of nature was especially evident in the mystery cults in which he attempted "to burst through the barrier that separates him from the universe of living things, to intensify the life feeling in himself to the point of liberating himself from his generic or individual *particularity.*"[15]

For Cassirer, mythical thinking was only the beginning of our present knowledge; as man gradually began to see things in abstract, or ideal terms, mythical thought gave way to scientific thought. Cassirer's implied conclusion—that mythical thought is inferior to scientific thought—has been criticized by a number of contemporary anthropologists. Chief among these critics is Claude Lévi-Strauss, who is convinced that

> the kind of logic in mythical thought is as rigorous as that of modern science . . . the difference lies, not in the quality of the intellectual process, but in the nature of the things to which it is applied . . . we may be able to show that the same logical processes operate in myth as in science, and that man has always been thinking equally well; the improvement lies not in an alleged progress of man's mind, but in the discovery of new areas to which it may apply its unchanged and unchanging powers.[16]

Artaud would agree neither with Lévi-Strauss nor with Cassirer, since he considers mythical thought *superior* to scientific thought, and even demands that we abolish all distinctions between mind and matter, between empty form and concrete being. Until now, says Artaud, European artists, lost in the seeming duality of matter and mind, have been unable to make contact with spiritual truths. Artaud wants them to understand that the spiritual and the material, the soul and the body, are both attributes of the same forces. They must perceive that the forces of the body and the mind are one and the same, and that a unique stream of energy permeates all of nature so that nothing is purely physical or purely spiritual. "According to the teachings of the great monastic philosophy, the forces of the Universe . . . are neither physical nor mental; sometimes they seem mental, and sometimes physical, according to the way in which you want to use them." (M, 72)

Many of the domains to which Artaud was attracted—astrology, alchemy, numerology, and magic—reflect the inability of mythical thought to distinguish between matter and its attributes, the whole and its parts, or between an object and its place in a temporal or spatial sequence. Alchemy is a good example of mythical thought in that it regards bodies as composed of attributes which, in themselves, can assume concrete existence. Hence, it confuses material substances and immaterial attributes. Many of Artaud's works, such as *La coquille et le clergyman* and *"Le théâtre et l'alchimie"* (in *Le théâtre et son double*), reflect his fascination with the alchemical process. Numerology and astrology, both of which play an essential role in *Les nouvelles révélations de l'être*, exerted a similar attraction upon him. Lastly, the sacred role that mythical thought assigns to spatial areas, as well as the objects they encompass, is mirrored in Artaud's praise of the Tarahumara "spatial" culture: "There is in this culture an idea of space, and I say that true culture can only be learned in space. . . . Culture in space means the culture of a mind which does not cease to breathe and to feel itself live in space." (T, 202)

Artaud shares primitive man's belief that all things in the world are interrelated, and that, as a consequence, a rapport exists between man and nature. Once we understand that our inner forces must vibrate in harmony with the universe, we will return to our true position in the cosmos. But, declares Artaud, our decadent European civilization, which has lost touch with natural forces, can only be saved by its artists. Following in the path of Rimbaud and Baudelaire, Artaud attributes visionary powers to artists; only they can pierce the veil of day-to-day reality and see the hidden universal forces which rule the world. Artists must discover "the analogical forces by means of which man's organism functions in accordance with the organism of nature. . . . And insofar as science and poetry are one and the same, this involves poets and artists, as well as scientists, even as it did in the time of the Popul Vuh." (M, 71) Like Renaissance man, Artaud believes that art, as is the case with science, constitutes one form of knowledge; and man must use all aspects of whatever knowledge he possesses in his quest for metaphysical truths. Man resembles everything else in the universe in that he is part of nature and is thereby governed by cosmic forces. Modern man may refuse to understand his relationship to nature, but primitive man was deeply aware of his cosmic role:

> From the beginning the ancient religions have wanted to glimpse the Great All. Ever since the genesis of the elements, they neither separated the sky from man, nor man from the entire creation. And it can even be said that, at the beginning, they clearly understood creation. (VII, 62)

The mythical thinking of primitive man obviously appealed to Artaud for its lack of abstraction. It was to be expected that Artaud, a man who was unable to order his thought impulses in a rational manner or to make his thought and being coincide, would welcome a mode of thinking which ignored abstractions and refused to separate thought and being. But mythical thought attracted him for another, and still more important, reason—one which was rooted in his ever-present mystical desires. In mythical thought, man is reduced to the level of all other things in the universe. Along with all animate and inanimate beings, he is subject to universal laws whereby his life is ruled by space, number, and time—in short, by destiny. Although Artaud professed a desire to control and determine himself, he was only too happy to relinquish his intelligence and free will whenever the opportunity arose. During the 1930's, he eagerly allowed destiny to play the same role that he had formerly assigned to Heloise and the clairvoyant. He happily submits to the laws of destiny, in the hope that he will be swept along by universal forces and thus lose all consciousness of his individual self. Paradoxically enough, he can only escape from his helplessness and impotence by yielding to a will more powerful than his own.

Artaud's conception of the theater reveals the intensity of his mystical longings. He shares Nietzsche's belief that the theater offers man the opportunity to unite with the Oneness of Being in a Dionysian frenzy. He wants the contemporary theater to introduce us into the very womb of Nature as did the Greek mysteries.

> The theater must become the equal of life—not of individual life, of this individual aspect of life where CHARACTERS triumph—but of a sort of liberated life, which sweeps away human individuality so that man is nothing more than a reflection. The true purpose of theater is the creation of Myths and the expression of the immense, universal side of life. (IV, 139)

Artaud finds the metaphor of the plague attractive because, for him, the plague is not a physical disease but a psychic entity resembling destiny; the plague is "the direct instrument of materialization of an intelligent force in close contact with what we call fatality." (IV, 22)

Since the ideal theater envisioned by Artaud is clearly metaphysical, it is understandable that Artaud should disparage the social, psychological theater of the West in favor of Oriental drama which concerns itself with spiritual realities. Orientals have understood that the language of the stage must correspond to movements of nature; their theater demonstrates that man and nature can form a perfect, harmonious whole. The individual, as such, ceases to exist as he is absorbed into universal life. In the Oriental theater, the actors' gestures reflect cosmic motions, the sound of the human voice corresponds to natural sounds, and all merge in an ultimate reality so that man and nature become one and the same:

> And the most commanding correspondences constantly join sight to sound, intellect to sensibility, the gesture of a character to the evocation of a plant's movements across the cry of an instrument. The sighs of a wind instrument prolong the vibrations of vocal cords with a sense of such oneness that you do not know whether it is the voice itself which continues or the oneness which has absorbed the voice from the beginning. (IV, 67)

The Oriental theater unveils spiritual truths and cosmic forces; it dares to contend with the "anguish of a soul which is the prey of phantasms from the Beyond." (IV, 78) By placing man in contact with spiritual realities, it produces the struggle our soul must wage in its efforts to reach "nirvana." (Buddhists consider that "nirvana" occurs when the soul detaches itself from the sphere of finite things and is annihilated even as it unites with a higher reality.) Balinese dancers, in touch with transcendent principles, lose all free will and behave like automatons controlled by all-powerful forces: "A kind of terror seizes us when we think of these mechanical beings; their joys and sorrows do not belong to them, but appear to follow age-old rituals which seem dictated by higher intelligences. In the last analysis, what strikes us most in this spectacle is this impression of a higher and prescribed life." (IV, 70) Evidently, Artaud would relish being one of those performers whose every movement is dictated by "higher intelligences." At the same time that the theater annihilates all individual will power and responsibility, it frees man of his body. By becoming a magic, sacred ritual, the theater allows him to reach a state of mystical ecstasy in which all awareness of earthly things disappears. Artaud has no doubt that the theater's task is to "liberate us from human contingencies."

The parallel drawn by Artaud between the theater and alchemy stems from his belief that the essential nature of both phenomena is mystical. Today, one thinks of alchemy in terms of a search for gold, but alchemy was originally associated with the quest for divine spiritual principles. Gold served as a material representation of spirituality. As Kurt Seligman observes, "The transmutation of base metals into gold was accomplished by another transmutation, that of man, and the seven steps, or stages, of the alchemical process were the symbols decking the path to blessedness. In this struggle, the alchemist sought a union of soul and mind with the divine."[17] According to Artaud, the action of the theater is analogous to the alchemical process because alchemy attempts to purify everything to arrive at gold (which represents spirituality), and the theater seeks to lead us to absolute purity.

> By the immensity of the conflicts it provokes, by the prodigious number of forces it arouses and hurls against each other, by this appeal to a sort of quintessential rekindling, which is brimming over with the consequences and charged with spirituality, the theatrical operation of making gold ultimately evokes in the spirit an absolute and abstract purity, beyond which there can be nothing. (IV, 62)

This moment of absolute purity resembles both the mystical moment of divine union and the Surrealist "point" in which all contradictions are resolved. Elaborating upon his comparison of alchemy with the theater, Artaud asserts that alchemical symbols are the spiritual counterpart of a material operation, while the theater is the counterpart of a hidden reality, one which is "dangerous and archetypal, where principles, like dolphins, show their heads and then hurry to return into the darkness of the waters." (IV, 58–59) Although Artaud tends to interpret "the theater's double" in varying ways, it is always clear that he has some form of transcendent reality in mind. For Nicola Chiaromonte, this double is "the incorporeal or transcendent essence of existence and its ultimate meaning."[18]

Much has already been said of esotericism in *Héliogabale*. Artaud's version of the historical rise and fall of the Roman emperor reveals his own mystical longings and desire for self-annihilation. In the belief that the ancient Syrians, like the Tarahumara, were in touch with metaphysical principles, Artaud asserts that these "pagans" were closer to the divine than modern man can ever hope to be. "What distinguishes the pagans from us is that at the origin of all their beliefs there is a terrific effort not to think as men, in order to stay in contact with the entire creation, that is, with the divinity." (VII, 60–61) The Syrians understood that they could not think of themselves as individuals if they wanted to remain in touch with metaphysical forces and unite with the Oneness of Being.

Artaud manages to interpret even Heliogabalus' cruelty in mystical terms. The emperor, Artaud tells us, did not indulge in cruelty for its own sake; rather, he inaugurated a reign of terror and anarchy in an attempt to reach a moment of essential unity. For, says Artaud, Heliogabalus understood that unity is perforce preceded by anarchy and disorder. Then too, the fact that the Syrians had multiple gods would, at first, seem to indicate that they did not comprehend the Oneness of all Being. However, Artaud resolves this apparent contradiction by explaining that the names of their gods connoted essential forces—all of which constituted the whole of Being. "I say that these names named forces, ways of being, modalities of the great power of being which is separated into principles, essences, substances, and elements."

(VII, 62) Once Absolute Being is found, all these forces will unite and the different gods representing them will die. It is interesting that Artaud interprets phenomena which seem opposed to the concept of unity—such as anarchy and multiplicity—as steps on the road to mystical oneness.

The concept of Absolute Being whose attributes are known to man raises a fundamental problem which has been carefully examined in the sacred books of Eastern mysticism and in the Cabala, the bible of Jewish mysticism, which also had a great influence upon Artaud. The problem is, basically, as follows: How can Absolute Being remain intact and distinct from the world and still manifest itself through its various forces which act *in* the world. In the Upanishads alone, at least two schools of thought exist on this question.

> The first is upheld by those who regard the world as real and therefore describe Brahman as its omnipotent and omnipresent Creator, Sustainer and Destroyer; such a Brahman is, to be sure, Saguna, endowed with attributes. But according to the opposite opinion, the world of names and forms is finally unreal and only Brahman exists. All that is perceived anywhere is Brahman alone, and this Brahman is unconditioned, free from all qualities or attributes. Thus the same indefinable Reality is described in two different ways according to the point of view of the perceiver.[19]

Faced with this same question, the Cabala attempts to resolve it in a different way. The Zohar, one of the most important books of the Cabala, distinguishes between two worlds which both represent God. One is primary and intelligible only to God (En-Sof), but is joined to the other one which makes it possible to know God since it is composed of attributes with which man comes into contact.[20] Artaud was aware of the intricate nature of this problem and of the solutions suggested in the Upanishads and in the Cabala. In *Héliogabale*, Artaud offers his own solution: All is a mani-

festation of Absolute Being, yet the Absolute needs nothing
—"Neither god, nor angel, nor man, nor mind, nor principle,
nor matter, nor continuity." (VII, 66) Justifying this statement, he explains that just as different objects create an idea
of matter, different beings give us an intimation of Absolute
Being.

Artaud's trip to Mexico was prompted in large part by
his spiritual longings; in the wilds of the New World Artaud hoped to find men who were still in communion with
natural and supernatural forces—men who had remained in
touch with the gods. The cosmic secrets guarded by the
Mexican Indians could inject new life into crumbling
Europe.

> Any true culture is based on race and blood. The Indian
> blood of Mexico preserves an ancient secret of race, and
> before the race is lost, I think we must obtain from it the
> power of this ancient secret. . . . The rationalist culture of
> Europe has failed, and I have come to the earth of Mexico
> to seek the basis of a magic culture which can still spring
> forth from the power of the Indian soil. (T, 182)

Once in Mexico, Artaud set out to locate the Tarahumara
tribe largely because of what he had heard about their peyote
rituals. The quest was successful and Artaud joined the Indians in attaining, through peyote, moments of mystical
ecstasy. The essay *"Le rite du peyote"* (in *Les Tarahumaras*)
describes the Indian belief that peyote enables man's soul
to re-enter into its original communion with the divine, a
communion lost in the course of the soul's sojourn on earth.
According to Artaud, the influence of the drug is such that
the Indian user loses all consciousness of his personality. Convinced that all is dictated by a superior force named Ciguri,
he renounces all control over mind and body. "If the Indian
is an enemy of his body, he also seems to have sacrificed his

consciousness to God." (T, 16) Distinguishing carefully between a man who deliberately allows peyote to affect him,
and a madman who loses all self-control, Artaud asserts that
only the former is conducted to a higher awareness of his
essential being. His will has been strengthened only after
he gives up the attempt to dominate himself:

> His personal consciousness has grown during this process of
> inner separation and division caused by peyote, a process
> which strengthens his will. If he seems to understand much
> better what he isn't than what he is, on the other hand,
> he knows what and who he is much better than we ourselves
> know what we are and what we want. (T, 17)

Under the influence of peyote a man perceives what ideas
he must accept to achieve a state of harmony, to feel himself free and unconstrained. His mind will intuitively know
"the thoughts and feelings that it can profitably welcome
without danger, and those which could harm the exercise
of his liberty." (T, 33) Echoing a now familiar theme, Artaud finds still one more reason to justify his willingness to
renounce any attempt at self-control. Equating liberty with
the *inability* to govern himself, he praises the drug-provoked
mystical experience in which all individuality is annihilated.
In *México,* Artaud takes a further step and insists that the
extinction of individual consciousness should form the base
of a new culture and civilization.

Many of the Tarahumara beliefs and rituals resemble
those aspects of Hindu and Orphic mysticism which had
attracted Artaud earlier in his career. The Hindu belief that
the soul will undergo successive incarnations until it re-
unites with the One divine Being finds a parallel in the
Tarahumara culture. The Indians are convinced that the soul
is but a reflection of infinite forces, and, under the influence
of peyote, can be brought back to the Infinite. And the fol-

lowers of Orpheus who sought to understand cosmic laws can be seen as the spiritual ancestors of the Tarahumara, who attempt to discover the secrets of the universe through their peyote rituals. If properly conducted, their rituals enable the Indians to comprehend the nature of the Universe, of Creation, and of God. "For the Ciguri Ritual is a creation Ritual which explains how things *exist* in the void and how the void exists in Infinity, and how things came out into Reality, and were created." (T, 23) Both the Orphic mysteries and the peyote rituals are intended to free man's soul from its bodily prison and allow it to communicate with the Infinite. Under the influence of the drug,

> you are no longer aware of the body that you have just left —a body whose very limits were reassuring. But, on the other hand, far greater happiness comes from belonging to the unlimited than to yourself because you understand that whatever the self was, it came from the fountainhead of that unlimited, from the Infinity which you are going to see. (T, 31)

Artaud welcomes the drug for a number of reasons: It permits superior powers to control his existence, it enables him to escape from his body, and it creates a self which is free of unwanted instincts. "Peyote brings the self back to its true sources. . . . And the whole series of lewd phantoms formed by the subconscious can no longer bully the true breath of MAN, for the good reason that it is not MAN as he is born, but INNATE man." (T, 33) The implication here is that "innate" man is free of violent, uncontrollable instincts. This passage provides a foretaste of the obsession with purity that runs throughout the poems Artaud wrote toward the end of his life.

It is clear that Artaud's mystical desires remained fairly constant throughout the 1920's and 1930's, although he

gradually ceased to speak of Eastern mysticism and turned
his energies first toward the theater, which, for him, was
an instrument of metaphysical communion, and then toward the Tarahumara civilization. His approach to language
also followed a consistent pattern in the course of these two
decades: an initial distrust of verbal language grew increasingly stronger and culminated in his conviction that our
language had to be radically transformed. He firmly believed
that a "cultural revolution," involving a return to mythical
thought, had to be accompanied by a new kind of language.
No doubt many of the linguistic ideas he espoused in the
1930's can be traced back to his affiliation with the Surrealists. In the belief that the language we use both reflects
and shapes our way of thinking, Breton had declared that
language had to be used "surrealistically" before a metamorphosis of contemporary society could be effected. Like
the Surrealist leader, Artaud sought a primitive language
which remained in touch with the being of things. He hoped
that the magical powers of such a language would reveal
metaphysical truths and allow us to re-establish a culture in
touch with divine principles. In his quest for such a language Artaud was led to explore a number of fundamental
problems relating to the nature and meaning of language
and poetry. Convinced that ordinary, discursive language
distorts ideas and emotions, Artaud asked when and how did
this language come into being. Was there ever a more primordial language which coincided directly with thought and
sensations? Was such a primordial language poetic or physical? Could it be re-created today? In the hope of finding
man's "original language," Artaud began to delve ever more
deeply into the secrets of poetic creation.

Many of the questions Artaud raised in this matter strike
a familiar note. Several of his linguistic theories, as well as
his ideas concerning primitive culture and myth, were in

the air in the 1920's and, in fact, had already been set forth by certain philosophers. A number of critics have already indicated the parallels that can be drawn between Nietzsche's concept of the theater and that of Artaud. Since Nietzsche was well-known in Surrealist circles, it is fair to assume that, directly or indirectly, he influenced Artaud. Also, many of Artaud's ideas on "authentic" language and poetry bring to mind Martin Heidegger, who was formulating many of his most important philosophical concepts in the 1920's. Like Artaud, Heidegger believes that the decadence in European culture can be traced to a degeneration of language. Convinced that an authentic or original language existed in pre-Platonic times, Heidegger maintains that such a language, unlike ordinary language, does not act as a "sign" for objects and ideas; on the contrary, real or authentic language actually brought things into being by differentiating them from everything else: "For words and language are not wrappings in which things are packed for the commerce of those who write and speak. It is in words and language that things first come into being and are."[21] With this original language, man delved into "unconcealment" and forced the universe to reveal itself. By discovering things through naming them—and hence, through language—man played an essential role in their creation. And, because language was instrumental in the creation of things, it was intimately related to being.

Pre-Platonic philosophers understood the fundamental relationship between the being of things and the words denoting them. But, laments Heidegger, the history of Western philosophy shows that being and language have been torn asunder with the result that idea and form have come to be regarded as separate entities. As language became purely abstract and logical, words were seen as "signs" for objects and ideas. Words began to conceal, rather than disclose, reality:

"Originally an act of violence that discloses being, the word sinks from this height to become a mere sign, and this sign proceeds to thrust itself before the essent."[22] Language started to conceal the being of things when the word began to "stand" for the reality. The results were disastrous; through language, Western man alienated himself from the true roots of being. The only language, according to Heidegger, which has remained in touch with primordial forces, is that of poetry. By uncovering the being of everything that exists, poetry preserves the authentic function of language—revelation. When poetry brings things into the open, it renders all language possible.

> Afterward it became clear that poetry is the inaugural naming of being and of the essence of all things—not just any speech, but that particular kind which for the first time brings into the open all that which we then discuss and deal with in everyday language. Hence poetry never takes language as a raw material ready to hand, rather it is poetry which first makes language possible.[23]

In revealing being, poetry performs the function of true language—a function that can never be fulfilled by logical, discursive language.

Like the German philosopher, Artaud attributed the sterility and decadence of European culture to our tendency to think in terms of signs and systems; as words became signs for things themselves, language distorted reality: "If confusion is the sign of the times, I see at the root of this confusion a rupture between things and the words, ideas, and signs which represent them." (IV, 12) Artaud's rejection of abstractions and logical systems is similar to Heidegger's conviction that such modes of thought and language are "inauthentic." For Artaud, abstract thought implies reflection. And since, as he asserts, reflection is derivative in nature it cannot possibly coincide with actual being. Unfortunately, says Artaud, Western man has come to equate the state of being civilized with thinking in terms of abstractions and systems. To quote a key passage once again: "A civilized man is judged by his behavior and he thinks the same way he behaves, but the very word 'civilized' invites confusion: everyone thinks that a cultured, civilized man is one who knows about systems and who thinks in systems, forms, signs and representations." (IV, 12–13)

The inadequacies Artaud found in logical, discursive language led him to espouse both poetry and "physical" language. During the 1920's Artaud's attitude toward paintings and films had made it clear that he preferred a visual language to a verbal one. In the following decade his concept of a visual language expanded until he found himself repeatedly expounding the merits of "physical," or "spatial," language. Best able to envision such a language in theatrical terms, Artaud declared that every idea and emotion presented on stage must be evoked by sounds, objects, decor, lighting, and costumes—in short, by all that is non-verbal. "I say that the stage is a physical, concrete place which asks to be filled and to be given a concrete language to speak." (IV, 45) This concept of "theater as spectacle" or "total theater," in which the spoken word plays a relatively minor role, has exercised an enormous influence on the contemporary stage. Artaud's attraction to physical language stems from his belief that, unlike ordinary language which distorts reality because it is reflective and abstract, physical language actually coincides with being.

At times, Artaud banishes discursive language from the theater by declaring that words must be used for their sound rather than for their meaning. Once stripped of their rational significance, words would serve the same function as musical notes or different shades of light and color. Artaud was convinced that the pitch of the voice, the repetition of certain syllables, could affect our nervous system and so influence us emotionally. If sounds, noises and cries are chosen first for their vibratory quality and only secondly for their meaning, language will communicate physically—not intellectually, and therefore superficially.

> Rhythmic repetition of syllables and special vocal modulations, which veil the precise sense of words, evoke multiple images in the brain, [and thereby] create a more or less hallucinatory state, and force the sensibility and the mind to undergo a kind of organic alteration which helps rid written poetry of its customary gratuitousness. (IV, 145)

Since Artaud often equated man's being with his physical existence, his desire that the theater address itself to the senses rather than the mind is understandable. He proposed to "treat the spectators like snakes to be charmed, and to evoke the subtlest ideas in them by means of their organisms." (IV, 97–98) His belief that words should be selected for their physical effects led him to admire the use of incantations in the Balinese theater.

In addition to sounds, lighting and physical objects, Artaud wanted actors' bodies to convey ideas. In a section of *Le théâtre et son double* titled *"Un athlétisme affectif"* ("An Emotional Athleticism"), Artaud utilizes Cabalistic notions to show that every feeling and every idea corresponds to, and can be manifested by, certain motions of the body and patterns of breathing. He even asserts that if this language of gesture and breath were to be presented on stage it would be universally comprehensible; verbal language, on the other hand, can be understood by only a limited number of people. "Without doubt, an appropriate breath corresponds to every feeling, to every mental movement, to every leap of human emotion." (IV, 155) But this concept raises a fundamental problem. If every gesture or breath corresponds to an idea or feeling, then we are plunged back into the realm of a pre-established system of signs and meanings; in other words, we are back in the same realm in which verbal language operates. While objects, sounds, and lighting may not "represent" or "mean" anything, the same cannot be said for a language of gestures. If a language of gestures were to limit itself to the evoking of basic emotions, then it would be easily, and perhaps universally, comprehensible. However, if, as Artaud seems to indicate, gestures correspond to specific feelings and ideas, then it would be necessary to know the "meaning" of each gesture. In this way, gestures, like words, would act as "signs" and consequently would share all the defects of verbal language. Jerzy Grotowski, director of the Polish Laboratory Theater, observes that Artaud's theory of gestures "would inevitably lead to stereotyped gestures destined to signify definite emotions."[24] Aware of this fundamental dilemma, Artaud insisted that he would reject the customary kind of pantomime in which particular gestures represent established concepts or ideas. Instead, he envisaged a "non-perverted" pantomime:

> By "non-perverted pantomime" I mean direct pantomime where gestures—instead of representing words or groups of sentences (as in our European pantomime) . . . represent ideas, mental attitudes and aspects of nature in an effective and concrete manner which involves the constant evoking of natural objects and details, as in the Oriental language which represents night by a tree upon which a bird, which had already closed one eye, begins to close the other. (IV, 48)

But is such a "non-perverted" pantomime possible? The example chosen by Artaud would seem to indicate that it is not, for the "sleeping bird" is quite definitely a "sign" for night.

It would seem that what Artaud really desires is not an end to language as such, but an end to verbal language. Such a sustained attack on words is not surprising coming, as it does, from a man who complained that he could neither complete his thought impulses nor make his words express adequately his most insignificant ideas and feelings. In fact, throughout *Le théâtre et son double* Artaud constantly praises concrete, physical language in order thereby to denigrate the value of words. He attacks written words with particular relish: "We must get rid of the superstitions attached to texts and *written* poetry. Written poetry is worth reading once, and then should be destroyed." (IV, 93–94) At times, however, his tone is less categorical and, instead of denouncing verbal language, he attempts to demonstrate its worthlessness. It is at these times that he brings Heidegger to mind. Like the German philosopher, he declares that the words we use distort the actual being of things. Since these words have been constantly borrowed and endlessly repeated, as they are handed down from one generation to another, they have gradually become emasculated, losing all contact with reality. Therefore, declares Artaud, no word is to be used twice.

> Let us leave textual criticism to students and formal criticism to esthetes, and recognize that what has been said does not remain to be said. An expression does not have the same value twice, nor does it live twice. Any word, once spoken, is dead and functions only at the moment of utterance. . . . The theater is the only place in the world where a gesture, once made, can never be made again. (IV, 90–91)

Artaud's assertion that a gesture cannot be made twice brings us back to the dilemma just discussed. Although it is true that gestures cannot be transmitted in written form, they *can* nevertheless become as stereotyped and empty as words.

As further argument against verbal language, Artaud maintains that words are incapable of expressing many states of being which can only be evoked or suggested in other ways. Convinced that the inaccuracy and the paucity of the words we use prevent our thoughts and our being from fully developing, he voices his belief "that words do not mean everything, and that because of their nature and characteristic rigidity . . . they arrest and paralyze thought instead of permitting and aiding its development." (IV, 132) Fundamental states of being lie hidden to us because we lack the words to describe and evoke them. If the theater can transcend the limitations of words, it will discover ideas and feelings unknown to us. "The idea of a play—made directly on stage—which encounters obstacles of staging and performance compels the discovery of a language—both active and anarchic—in which the usual limits of feelings and words are pushed aside." (IV, 49)

Not only is verbal language unable to express man's inner reality; it is also incapable, says Artaud, of revealing metaphysical truths. He believes that physical language transmits spiritual signs which "can be understood intuitively but never translated into logical discursive language." This assumption, however, raises a number of problems. Even if language could transcend the limitations imposed by words, there is no reason to conclude that it would necessarily become "metaphysical." Secondly, why is physical language better suited to evoke cosmic realities than words? While it is true that the spiritually oriented Eastern theater employs pantomime, this does not mean that by using pantomime the Western theater will thereby automatically be able to evoke metaphysical truths. As Nicola Chiaromonte observes, "Pantomime does not lead to the 'metaphysical' theater of rigorous moral purity envisaged in *Le théâtre et son double*."[25]

Artaud's burning desire to create a physical language in the theater was to be constantly frustrated in the course of his attempts to produce plays for the Théâtre de la Cruauté. It was only later—during his trip to Mexico—that he believed he had finally found the language he so ardently sought. For Artaud, the mountains and the terrain where the Tarahumara tribe made its home were strewn with natural "signs" and "symbols," suggesting emotions and ideas. The configurations of the landscape constituted a form of physical language employed by Nature herself to communicate with man.

> The land of the Tarahumara is full of signs, forms and natural effigies which do not seem to have been born accidentally; [rather, it is] as if the gods, who seem omnipresent here, had wished to manifest their powers through these strange signatures . . . it's as if Nature *had wanted to speak* on the *geographic area of a race*. (T, 43)

Artaud finds the language of the Tarahumara mountains doubly satisfying: it is both metaphysical, since it has been created by powers superior to man, and non-verbal.

Once again, it is evident that Artaud does not reject "signs" and "symbols" as such, but only *verbal* "signs." He is perfectly content to have natural configurations "represent" ideas, even if the ideas in question are as abstract as the concept of universal duality. He does not doubt, for example, that certain trees "have been *deliberately* burned into the form of crosses, or of beings; these beings are often double and face one another, as if to manifest the essential *duality* of things." (T, 47) Statements such as this lead one to think that Artaud, by projecting his own ideas of metaphysics onto the natural landscape, falls into the trap of the pathetic fallacy. Otto Hahn finds that "the rocks and landscapes in *D'un voyage au pays des Tarahumaras* have the same appearance as the 'Theater of Cruelty': Indians tied up, tortured bodies. Seeking signs everywhere, he [Artaud] projects his own meanings, and his own hopes."[26]

Les Tarahumaras, like *Le théâtre et son double,* contains numerous passages in which Artaud attempts to prove the superiority of physical language. He constantly repeats the argument that verbal language, reflective and abstract by nature, can never coincide with acts, things, or ideas. An idea expressed by words is already a thing of the past, for thought can never coincide with language. "What we place in front of us so that reason can look at it, is, in reality, already the past; and reason holds nothing but a form, more or less empty, of true thought." (T, 184–185)

Despite the fact that his recurring praise of physical language is invariably accompanied by a condemnation of words, Artaud at times appears willing to use verbal language. He makes it clear, for example, that he would welcome words provided they conveyed the meaning they possessed at their origin when they were in actual contact with the roots of being. "And I claim the right to break with the usual meaning of language, to split its backbone once and for all . . . to return to the etymological origins of language which . . . always evoke a concrete notion." (IV, 121) But such a desire is not easily attained. It is often impossible to determine the etymological meaning of a word, even if one makes the rather dubious assumption that words and being were originally one and the same. Further, since the meaning of words has often changed radically in the course of their evolution, isn't it possible, and even probable, that the audience will not understand what is being said? Lastly, how can one interrupt a dramatic presentation, which is intended to have a physical effect upon the spectator, with a digression on the meaning of words?

Artaud recommends, also, that the theater use words as they appear in dreams. But this too creates problems. As Nicola Chiaromonte points out:

> What does it mean to give words uttered on the stage the importance they have in dreams? It implies either a recitation of senseless phrases in somnambulistic attitudes, or the opposite: a stylized, lyrical performance with words sounding as if they were dreamed, only because they take on a surrealistic quality entirely different from their value in ordinary discourse.[27]

And, continues the critic, if words were to be used in this lyrical manner, they would have to be carefully chosen in advance. Yet Artaud himself consistently opposed the use of preselected words and a written text.

Far more important than Artaud's theories concerning etymological or dreamlike language was his espousal of poetry. The emphasis Artaud places on poetry brings André Breton to mind. Like the Surrealist leader, Artaud maintains that real poetry penetrates to the core of Being by revealing occult truths through symbols and analogies. Convinced that words can actually change the course of reality, he shares Breton's belief that poetry is akin to magic. "We want to restore to poetry its dynamic and virulent meaning, its power as a magical thing. And this magic must be seen as an unleashing of real forces, in accordance with a kind of precise ritual." (IV, 281) Far more mystical, however, in his approach to poetry than Breton, Artaud denigrates lucid, discursive language. This, he says, destroys the great emotional feeling which renders possible both poetry and a spir-

itual "void." The void thus evoked by Artaud appears to
have definite affinities with the void which so many mystics
have sought to create in themselves so that they might become more receptive to spiritual truths.

> Any powerful feeling creates the idea of the void within us.
> And the lucid language which obstructs this void also pre-
> vents poetry from appearing in thought. This is why images,
> allegories, and figures [of speech] which mask what they
> want to reveal have far more significance for the mind than
> the lucidities accompanying articulated analyses. (IV, 86)

A number of Artaud's other works also speak of this spiritual
void and of its relationship to poetry. In *Les nouvelles
révélations de l'être* Artaud declares that he is forced to suffer
because he was too cowardly to accept the void within him:
"I know that they wanted to enlighten me by the Void and
that I refused to let myself be enlightened." (VII, 150) And,
in an essay written in Spanish, *"Secretos eternos de la Cul-
tura,"* he describes the Chinese belief that a void is at the
center of all things—a void which only poetry can enter.
"This void will never be filled by science; but poetry, seen
as a useful and rational means of divination, could be used
to establish the bases which will permit us to progress." (M,
84)

   In many ways, Artaud's conception of poetry is akin to
that of Nietzsche. The latter is not concerned with poetry
in general, but rather with dramatic poetry; for him the
theater's original purpose was to reveal man's place in a
chaotic, fluctuating universe. By reflecting essential movements of nature and primordial struggles, dramatic poetry
mirrored the cosmos. For this reason he believed that poetic
metaphors were more "real" than logical statements. Like
Artaud, Nietzsche demands that the theater lead us back to
concrete reality, and decries the fact that Western thought

has accorded an increasingly dominant role to abstract, logical thought: "Ever since Socrates the mechanism of concepts, judgments, and syllogisms has come to be regarded as the highest exercise of man's powers, nature's most admirable gift."[28] Emphasizing the mythopoeic structure underlying all drama, Nietzsche asserts that our relationship to the world can be instinctively apprehended only through an understanding of myth as it is expressed in poetry.

Although Artaud, like Nietzsche (and Breton), assigns a metaphysical role to poetry and myth, it is frequently unclear whether he is speaking of poetry in general or, more specifically, of dramatic poetry. Far more than any of his contemporaries, or predecessors, Artaud is preoccupied with the existence and function of anarchy in poetry—an interest not surprising in one who associated anarchy with violence and cruelty. Convinced that an anarchic universe existed before the creation of distinct forms or things, Artaud asserts that it is the mission of poetry to evoke such a universe; true poetry is always "Genesiacal and chaotic, and always has its roots in Genesis and Chaos. When poetry isn't somewhat anarchic, when it lacks fire and incandescence or the magnetic whirlwind of worlds in formation, it isn't poetry." (II, 251) By creating anarchy, poetry breaks through the crust of disembodied abstractions and logical statements that distort reality. Not only must poetry demolish our false conception of outer reality, it must enable us to perceive human nature in a new, more profound manner. In a statement reminiscent of Breton's Manifestoes of Surrealism, Artaud tells us that poetry will overturn all existing relationships "not only in the outer domain—that of nature—but in the inner domain, that is, in the domain of psychology." (V, 40) Artaud compares poetic anarchy to a form of humor embodied, for him, in the films of the Marx Brothers. He considers their humor "anarchistic" in that it destroys our belief in reality by demonstrating that accepted relationships could be completely otherwise. The theater, he asserts, must present this anarchy and humor in such manner that the spectator will find himself physically affected.

> These actual appearances of monsters, these debauches of heroes and gods, these plastic manifestations of forces and these explosive interventions—all of which are part of a humor and a poetry which are ready to disorganize and pulverize appearances according to the analogical, anarchistic principle of all genuine poetry—will only maintain their true magic in an atmosphere of hypnotic suggestion in which the mind is affected by the direct pressure felt by the senses. (IV, 149–150)

If the contemporary theater is decadent, it is so because it has lost all humor, all sense of "laughter's power of physical and anarchic disassociation"; it has "broken away from the spirit of profound anarchy which is at the root of all poetry." (IV, 51)

Passages in *Héliogabale* reveal the disquieting implications of Artaud's attitude toward poetic anarchy and violence. He was willing to condone any excesses, no matter how bloody, provided he saw in them some evidence of the anarchy he sought. In the light of the last fifty years of world history, such an attitude is obviously dangerous in terms of humanistic values. For, once again, Artaud conveys the impression that he welcomes violence for its own sake and only speaks of "anarchy" and "poetry" in an attempt at self-justification. For example, when he tells us that the cruelty practiced by Heliogabalus provoked a state of anarchy leading to poetry, he obviously relishes the gorier aspects of this anarchy. "And poetry, which restores order, first resuscitates disorder, a disorder full of inflamed elements; thrusting these elements against each other, it brings them to a single point of flames, gestures, blood and screams." (VII, 106) Artaud's-belief that the world must be reduced to this state of violent anarchy before a new order can be reborn brings to mind his espousal of catharsis by plague or by drama. It follows quite naturally that the violence created by the Roman emperor—like that of the plague—suggests the theater to Artaud. Assuring us that Heliogabalus introduced theater and poetry into his palace, Artaud goes on to declare that real poetry in the palace of a Roman emperor "deserves the shedding of blood." One cannot but conclude that either Artaud views anarchy and violence in terms that are purely metaphorical (which seems unlikely), or else he is unconcerned with the value of human life.

These extreme statements and this bloodthirsty attitude obviously stem from Artaud's personal difficulties—the same difficulties which led him to demand that both our culture and our language be transformed. However intense Artaud's problems, they did not affect the *way* he wrote in the 1930's. Despite his rejection of everyday language, none of the books of this period is at all radical in its approach to language. In fact, Artaud was clearly concerned with traditional questions of style in *Héliogabale* and in *Le théâtre et son double*, two works which are quite lyrical. It is only in the completely personal poems created during and after his stay at Rodez that Artaud's writing reflects his own dilemma and his preoccupations. In these poems, Artaud attempts to use language in a new way. Whether or not he was successful, whether it is possible for anyone to succeed in an undertaking of this kind, will be examined in the following chapter.

IV

RETURN
TO THE
BODY

Artaud's long Calvary, which took him from one mental institution to another, began in 1937. Virtually silent for nine years, upon his release in 1946 he began to write furiously, as if to make up for lost time. From 1946 until his death in 1948 he devoted all his energies to poetry, with the notable exception of his book on Van Gogh. For many readers of Artaud these poems constitute the most important part of his career. No longer does Artaud make use of universal terms to camouflage, or justify, his own problems, as he did in *Le théâtre et son double* and *Héliogabale*. Nor is there an effort to analyze the mechanism of his thoughts and the dilemma of his being, as he attempted to do at the outset of his career. His desperate attempts to dissect the nature of his problems have come to an end. Completely disillusioned with the value of intellectual analysis, he now seeks only to convey to us the intensity of his sufferings. His lifelong fears and hatreds, more intense than ever, are voiced in violent and often brutal terms. For Stephen Koch, Artaud's last poems "resemble the screams heard in the most up-to-date hospitals. They are assaults, and when really read, they are almost unendurable."[1]

The violence of these poems stems, at least partially, from Artaud's conviction that he is surrounded by enemies on all sides. Even as he attempts to fight them off he knows his efforts are doomed to failure. Threatened by one and all, he is convinced that inner and outer forces are conspiring to destroy him. Earlier feelings of persecution have given way to full-fledged paranoia. To quote Stephen Koch once more:

> This is poetry determined by an advanced stage of paranoia, directed against a loathed and invincible threat—a threat created, true enough, by Artaud himself, but nonetheless seen as external. Because it is alien, Artaud speaks to make contact with it; because it is loathed, he speaks with violence; because it is invincible, his awareness is limited to an unconfessed sense of futility which renders his expression both incomplete and unremitting.[2]

Artaud's sense of persecution leads him to identify with those Romantic poets who saw themselves the innocent victims of a ruthless society. The poets most often mentioned in Artaud's later works are Poe, Lautréamont, Baudelaire and Nerval—the *"poètes maudits"* of the nineteenth century whose lives ended in poverty, alcoholism, and madness. Espousing the Romantic belief that suffering must necessarily accompany true poetry, Artaud writes to Henri Parisot that "everything which is not tetanus of the soul or does not come from tetanus of the soul like the poems of Baudelaire and Edgar Allan Poe is not real and cannot be considered poetry." (R, 13–14) Unlike his spiritual predecessors, however, Artaud believed that suffering was, first and foremost, physical in nature. Convinced that physical suffering produces in the body a black lump of mucus, he asserted that since Coleridge lacked such a lump he couldn't have suffered; consequently, he could not have written great poems. Coleridge "wasn't a man who could produce this mucus in order to live, to live in immortality. Without doubt, the crime of the ancient mariner is that of Coleridge himself; the bird is this human soul which Coleridge killed in order to live." (SR, 28–29) That is, Coleridge had to compromise himself and kill whatever was immortal and unique within him in order to live in the everyday world.

Artaud adhered to the belief, held by many nineteenth-century writers, that the poet has access to a transcendent realm hidden to ordinary mortals. Society, he maintained, fears the revelations that spring from the poet's visionary powers. Men refused to listen to "Baudelaire, Edgar Allan Poe, Gérard de Nerval and the unthinkable comte de Lautréamont, out of fear that their poetry would leap forth from the printed page and overthrow reality." (LL, 8) Because of its fears, society deliberately tortures the poet. This phenomenon was understood by Coleridge, who saw that "priests, initiates, gurus, scholars, together with the complicity of the showcase doctor and the yogi behind his screens, never cease their secret flogging of the suffering poet's true heart." (SR, 26) Artaud's experience in mental hospitals reinforced his belief that the man of genius is always persecuted. In *Van Gogh, le suicidé de la société,* he places the burden of guilt on society's doctors, declaring that psychiatry was invented as a defense against visionaries. On occasion, Artaud's fears reach hysterical heights. He is obviously terror-stricken that the parasitic beings which destroyed Lautréamont will descend upon him. "I mean that he [Lautréamont] and his soul were surrounded by these germ-infested flakes, this slobbering acrimonious onrush of all the most sordid parasites of being and all the ancient ghosts of non-being." (LL, 9)

Artaud's belief that the poet is in touch with a transcendent realm indicates that his mystical longings are still very much with him. But his later poems make it clear that these longings have undergone a strange transformation, which seems to have begun around the same time that he re-entered the Catholic Church during his trip to Ireland. Many Catholic doctrines were given new interpretation in Artaud's obsessed mind. Not only did he literally believe in the reality of angels and devils, he often declared that he himself was Christ and had come to earth to save mankind. At times, he would maintain that Christ had come to earth in the person of Artaud. Toward the end of his stay at Rodez he rejected Catholicism and, along with it, all schools of religious and philosophical thought. But although he repeatedly denied the existence of supernatural phenomena, he continued to see demonic monsters on every side. Convinced that he was bewitched, he introduced incantations and exorcisms into his poetry to withstand the magic spells cast upon him. Nothing he did, however, succeeded in dissipating the vampires and incubi preying upon him, and much of the violence of his later poems reflects a desperate attempt to rid himself of these evil spirits.

His former attraction to the great metaphysical books of mankind—the Upanishads, the Cabala, the Tibetan and Egyptian books of the dead—has given way to a furious hatred of them and the men who created them. As in the case of Lautréamont and Baudelaire before him, his blasphemy is partly the result of disappointed spiritual longings. Artaud does not spare any religion—of the East or the West. In two articles published posthumously in *La Tour de Feu,* he derides the Hindu notion of yoga, asserting that the breath and spirit of man are not transcendent, and that "our backs are full of vertebras, which are stabbed by the nail of pain and which . . . teach us more about ourselves than any metaphysical or metapsychic research concerning the principle of life."[3] *Lettre contre la Cabbale,* as its title implies, attacks that great compendium of Jewish mysticism.

Artaud questions all its major doctrines, revealing in the process how well he had absorbed it. If God is innumerable, he asks, why do the Cabalists attempt to understand his nature by numbers? Why are certain numbers and combinations thereof thought to be mystical? Artaud now perceives that the idea of a divine plan, as set forth in the Cabala, has blinded us to the truth of reality. The Zohar, in fact, teaches nothing inasmuch as it deals with non-existent realities; things do not come from numbers, nor do they come from nothing. Artaud is not satisfied merely to expose the logical or intellectual inconsistencies in these books; he is also convinced that they are capable of harming humanity, especially himself. In fact, if he had not felt personally threatened, it is unlikely that he would have attacked them with such vehemence. Violently condemning all who claim to interpret the sacred books of the world, he tells us that "this somber and unknown group consistently uses the Cabala, the Zohar, the Sepher Yezirah, the Vedas, the Puranas, and the Ramayana to justify its misdeeds." (C) Elsewhere, he denigrates these sacred books by affirming that the mystical, contemplative states they advocate "are based on lewdness, which leads astray fundamental vigor."[4] But, the very fact that Artaud feels so menaced shows that, despite all his protestations to the contrary, he continues to believe in the power of these spiritual books and doctrines.

Artaud's denunciation of spirituality goes hand in hand with an utter rejection of mind and thought. After declaring that thought is an unnecessary superstructure of man ("thought is a matron which has not always existed" [I, 11]), he proclaims the joy he experiences upon reaching a realm where abstract ideas and rational thought no longer exist. "As a poet, I hear voices which are no longer from the world of ideas. For here where I am there is nothing more to be

thought." (I, 11) In this ideal world, knowledge—the de-
stroyer of life—is also banished. (Clearly, Artaud is referring
to conceptual, rational knowledge.) He has reached a stage
beyond knowledge, where everything simply *is:*

> there is no learning, no knowledge,
> life has been lost from the day that one single
> thing was known.
>
> I am not of your world,
>
> mine is on the other side of everything that is, knows and
> is aware of itself, desires and makes itself

(LS, 131)

Resolutely condemning any mental construction which attempts to alter the brute facts of reality, Artaud praises Van
Gogh for the latter's refusal to permit any philosophical or
intellectual ideas to distort his view of the world. In spite
of all pressures exerted upon him, Van Gogh managed to
remain in constant touch with life and nature; his paintings
reveal a world where there is "no soul, no mind, no consciousness, no thought, nothing but basic elements alter-
nately enchained and unchained." (VG, 60) The Dutch
painter had the genius to realize the great importance of
daily reality which is "frightfully superior to any history,
to any fiction, to any divinity." (VG, 29)

Artaud's rejection of the mind was not a new development:
Throughout his life he had repeatedly asserted that rational
thought could not seize fundamental aspects of life. In the
years immediately preceding his death, however, his attack
on the intellect grew more heated than ever. In a poem
written in March 1947, and called, appropriately enough,
"Chiote à l'esprit" ("Shit to the mind"), he rejects all literary,
religious and philosophical schools of thought which regard
the mind as superior to the body. Ideas, says Artaud, come

from the body, and not from the mind, which is nothing
more than a mere parasite:

> It's that the mind is pretentious and phony.
> A kind of larval smoke which only lives upon what it has
>   drawn out from
> the body struggling to make a gesture
> and not an idea or fact.
> For really, what are these ideas, facts, values and qualities?
> Lifeless terms which only become real when the body has
>   sweated them out.
>
> (CE, 6)

In *Ci-gît, précédé de la culture indienne*, Artaud takes a
further step. Not only does he insist that we must turn to
our sensory and physical experiences if we want to get at the
truth; he maintains that the mind was actually born of the
body.

> From the pain mined from the bone
> something was born
> which became what was mind
> to scrape around in the pain driven
> by pain
>   this womb
> a concrete womb
>   and the bone
>   the depths of the rock
>   which became bone

Artaud had formerly declared that ideas come from our
bodies, from the very marrow of our bones. But never before
had he advanced this thesis with such striking imagery.

For Artaud, immediate sensations, rather than conceptual
notions, constitute the only reality we can know. Once we
"think" about sensations, they lose all immediacy and we
begin to see them through a beclouded mental screen.

When my hand burns,
there is the fact that my hand burns which, considered
as a fact, is already in trouble,
having the feeling that my hand is burning means
entering another domain.

If I have the idea that my hand burns, I am no
longer in my hand but in a state of supervision.[5]

When man removes himself from his immediate physical
sensations by reflecting upon them, he encloses himself in
an illusory world of mental constructions, and all action
is halted.

Without feelings and ideas my hand could readily have
crushed the fire that a world of vicious and cowardly jealous
men, a world of lazy intellectuals, had created in order to
give itself a *"raison d'être,"* because feelings and the mind
have poisoned life.[6]

Artaud's praise of the body, and of the value of immediate
physical sensations, raises a major question. Because his body
—a source of pain and unwelcome instincts—had unfortunately had such a profound affect on his whole life, Artaud
had always longed to escape from the bonds of corporeality.
How could he then place such faith in the very body which
had always tormented him? Artaud resolved this apparent
contradiction in a very curious way: he turned on the mind
and attributed to it all the unpleasant functions and diseases normally associated with the body. By assigning to the
mind all the repugnant aspects of physical existence, he
"purified" the body. As Stephen Koch observes: "He ex-
ternalized his entirely modern intellect, attributed to it
everything loathesome usually associated with the body, and
assaulted it in a hitherto unknown poetry of the human
voice as pure action. Perhaps this new metaphor—the mind

as loathed physicality—is the most important aspect of Artaud's writings."[7] This "solution," however, led Artaud into still another ambiguity. In order to castigate and denounce the mind he was compelled to recognize its existence. And, this is precisely what he refused to do: his later poems continually declare that the mind does not exist. As we've noted, a similar logical impasse characterizes Artaud's attitude toward the supernatural: although he cries out that all spiritual phenomena are imaginary, he continues to live in fear of demonic creatures whom he can neither see nor hear.

Why does Artaud, possessed of a keen analytical mind, allow himself to fall into these obvious pitfalls of illogic? Such contradictory positions can stem only from intense fears and hatreds. Artaud's fear of evil spirits may have been such that he could obtain peace of mind only by continually refusing to admit their existence. Similarly, his hatred of the mind may have caused him both to heap invectives upon it and also to deny its very existence. Lastly, his assertions that the mind is nothing more than a parasite of the body grew more numerous in proportion to the intensity of his physical sufferings. Never had Artaud been in greater pain than during these years; his health had deteriorated while he was hospitalized and he was already suffering from the rectal cancer that was to prove fatal. In these circumstances it is not surprising that he should think only the world of the body was real, and that "the body is a fact which dispenses with ideas." Formerly, in order to feel he existed, Artaud split himself in two so that he could remain himself and yet see himself as another. But now—now that he is nothing but a body—he needs no one to reassure him of his being. "There is no inside, no mind, no outside or consciousness, nothing but the body just as you see it—a body whose existence doesn't cease even when the eye looking at it turns away. And this body is a fact: me."[8]

Since Artaud's ideas on the mind and its thought processes remained essentially unchanged throughout his life, it follows naturally that his attitude toward language and literature was equally consistent. In the course of the 1920's Artaud had repeatedly declared that true literature had to coincide with the deepest layers of man's being, with the very "stuff of the body." For this reason, he had questioned the value of rational, discursive language which, he felt, merely transcribed the most superficial aspects of human reality. Twenty years later these ideas remained essentially unchanged.

The preface Artaud wrote in 1947 for the proposed Gallimard edition of his collected works reveals the intensity of his hatred for conventional discursive language. In this, he categorically declares that henceforth he will write only for illiterates—for those who do not understand normal language. "But let my life's swollen words finally swell up by themselves from living in the a b c of writing. I am writing for illiterates." (I, 11) In *Ci-gît* Artaud goes even further and asserts that true language is incomprehensible. When Artaud says "incomprehensible," he undoubtedly means not explicable rationally or intellectually. Playing on the words *"claque"* and *"claque-dents"* (both of which mean "whorehouse" in slang), he writes:

> All true language
> is incomprehensible,
> like the clack
> of chattering teeth;
> or the clack (whorehouse)
> of the toothy femur (bloody).
>
> (*Tout vrai langage,
> est incompréhensible,
> comme la claque*

du claque-dents;
ou le claque [bordel]
du fémur à dents [en sang])

Condemning any work which intellectualizes sensations and emotions, Artaud proceeds to attack authors who cultivate a "style." He uses this word to designate a certain type of rarefied, lifeless literature (exemplified by the minor symbolists) in which the writer places an esthetic distance between himself and his work. Even his own early poems had been composed in a certain "literary style." Like the work of Marie Laurencin, Utrillo, and Raoul Dufy, these poems reveal "a furious impotence, like that of a dandy who would have his cuffs starched even though he had only the trunk of a guillotined man for a shirt collar." (I, 8)

Artaud had always believed life and literature to be necessarily inseparable. Once he became convinced that life itself could be reduced to physical terms, it was logical that he should want poetry to coincide with man's very body. He denounces the poems he wrote at the outset of his career because they ignored his physical being. "I have not been able to introduce my texture into these aborted poems, to introduce into their words not my soul, O not my soul, but my *pressure,* the darkness of my congenital tension, of my excessive and arid oppression." (I, 9) This "congenital tension" can be nothing other than his physical presence. Poetry must be one with the body, even if it must therefore partake of the body's most unpleasant functions. "When you dig into the *caca* of being and its language, the poem must necessarily smell bad." (R, 14) He admires the Surrealists because all aspects of physical being are found in their paintings and poetry. "I do not know what poets usually sing about, nor why, but the surrealistic poets do not sing: they bawl, yell, bleat, blow their noses, sneeze, cough, piss in their poetry; they walk and fart in it."[9]

When Artaud speaks of the identity that must exist between poetry and the body he almost invariably emphasizes the repugnant aspects of corporeality. Undoubtedly, this reflects his obsession with bodily functions and disease. But it is also true that Artaud wanted poetry to espouse the body in all its ugliness—an ugliness which, for him, forms the most fundamental substratum of our being—in the hope that it (i.e., poetry) would thereby become indissolubly welded to physical existence. Artaud's desire to unite poetry and the most loathsome aspects of physicality was most intense during his stay at Rodez. In one letter from Rodez, addressed to Henri Parisot, poetry becomes such an intimate part of man's sexuality that one cannot be certain whether Artaud is referring to a poem or to a penis. In the same breath, he urges that language be abandoned and that the flesh from man's sexual organ be stripped. The imagery employed is such that these two demands merge so that the act of creation becomes one with the sexual act. "It is all very well to abandon language and its laws in order to twist them, and to strip the sexual flesh from the glottis whence come the soul's seminal acidities and the moans of the unconscious, but only on condition that the sexual organ is seen as a rebel's orgasm—lost, naked, uterine and also piteous." (R, 15) In *"Coleridge le traître,"* poetry becomes a physical disease "played upon" a background of blood.

I say poetry poetry, poetic *consumptive* poetry,
pretty gasp on bloody red backdrop, the repressed depths
poemically, the poematic of the too-raw real.

For *afterward*, say *after* the "poematic" will come
the time of blood. Since *"ema,"* in Greek, means blood, and
po-ema must mean
afterward:
blood,
blood, afterward.

First let's make *poem,* with blood.

(SR, 25)

Artaud plays on "po-ema" to show that the word "poem" contains within it *"ema,"* the Greek word for blood. Since, in truth, Artaud actually believed in the reality of words and language, he was certain that poetry exists in the same way as do concrete things. Going one step further, he concluded that poetry is made from the very stuff—in this case, blood— that constitutes the body.

Although Artaud's desire to make poetry and the body coincide could never be literally realized, all of his later poems are strongly marked by the presence of the body: vivid metaphors of brutal physical sensations give to his poems a directness and a violence unequaled elsewhere in his work. Formerly, Artaud analyzed his reactions in intellectual terms. Now, however, his problems can no longer be *understood,* only *felt.* And, for the first time, his own work seems to meet his lifelong demand that literature have the power to move us viscerally rather than intellectually.

All his old obsessive anxieties are now revealed through metaphors. Instead of informing us, for example, that his being is menaced (as he would have done twenty years earlier), he evokes this sensation with physical, concrete images. His body is crushed while his mind is wrenched open and attacked.

> When the rock was eaten by the bone
> that the mind gnawed at from behind
> the mind opened its mouth too wide
> and received in the behind
> of the head
> a blow to wither its bones
> Then

> *then*
> then
> bone by bone
> the everlasting leveling returned.
>
> (CG)

The mind is no longer an instrument of thought and reflection but a hungry parasite preying upon the body. The "everlasting leveling" inspires Artaud with dread for he is afraid of being crushed. This is a fear which haunts him constantly; elsewhere, he looks in horror at a lewd sky slowly descending upon him.

> The anchored mind
> screwed into me
> by the sky's
> psycho-lascivious
> thrust
> is the one that imagines
> all temptations
> all desires
> all inhibitions
>
> (Momo, 9)

The bodily disintegration he suffers when he is crushed is conveyed by other metaphors. Among the many diseases most frequently mentioned is gangrene and its resultant rot and decomposition.

> Artaud
> who knew that there is no mind
> but a body
> which remakes itself like the gears
>   of a toothy corpse
> in the gangrene

                    of the femur
                        within.

                        (CG)

In *"Fragmentations"* (p. 680), Artaud associates gangrene
with the spiritual values he now abhors. He gives voice to
the fear that his body will disintegrate and his limbs crumble
away. "Morphine on a wooden leg, made, this morphine,
with the gangrene of the bones of the dead leg, then withdrawn,
that's what the holy trinity was."

His teeth and bones—two parts of his body which caused
him great pain—are particularly vulnerable. At one point,
Artaud indicts God for using his bones as a vantage point
from which to destroy his poetry.

                That means that there is a bone
                where
                                    god
                pounced upon the poet
                in order to plunder the ingestion
                of his poetry [*vers*]
                like farts of the head
                that he pulls out of him through the cunt
                                    (Momo, 13)

Artaud continued to regard God as a powerful enemy even
while he resolutely denied his existence. The word *"vers"*
could mean either "lines of poetry" or "worms." (Since Artaud
was nauseated by all bodily functions, including digestion,
it is entirely likely that he thinks of the food we have
eaten as "worms.") In either case, he is charging God with
robbing him of the nourishment—be it spiritual or material—he
needs in order to live.

Other physical images, equally brutal and horrifying, reveal
the sense of impotence Artaud suffered in his confrontation
with the world. He frequently envisaged himself as

bound and strangled. A dream described in *"Les malades et les médecins"* ("Patients and Doctors") depicts an Artaud trapped into complete helplessness. "By dint of sawing and grinding with my whole being in the midst of conspicuous sexuality, I understood that this spider's web was made of ropes and that these ropes, from the top of an abyss, held me back." (p. 18) This poem, like *Van Gogh, le suicidé de la société,* castigates doctors with great bitterness. His hatred of doctors and psychiatrists was so intense that one wonders whether he is speaking metaphorically when he accuses Van Gogh's psychiatrists of having suffocated their patient: "You decree that active consciousness is delirium but, nevertheless, you strangle it with your filthy sexuality." (VG, 13) Artaud's torture does not come to an end with suffocation and dismemberment; he is also crucified. He is being thus punished because he refused to submit to God and Jesus Christ, both of whom he regards as forces of evil. In the following poem, Artaud-the-helpless-patient has become Artaud-the-archetypal-victim.

and on the thumb
the spiked nail of the finger pointing to the nail
                              to be nailed
           that I am
since before eternity
that a hundred billion nails of shit began to
                nail down
by myriads of billions, huge numbers of myrmidons
                without end
on the wall of the infinite fugitive

                                        (84, 118)

(et sur le pouce
le cloue encloué de l'index indicateur du clou à clouer que
               je suis
depuis avant l'eternité

> *que cent milliards de clous de mouscaille se soient mis à*
>   *clouter*
> *par myriades de milliards de chiffres de mirmidons sans*
>   *fond*
> *sur la muraille de l'infini marron)*

Artaud enjoys multiple plays on words in this poem. The word "clou*e*," for example does not exist; however, *"enclouer"* refers to the injury done to a horse in the process of being shod, and *"encroué"* could mean hung or crucified. On another level of meaning, this poem is almost an exercise in underworld slang. An *"indicateur"* is a "stool pigeon," while a *"marron"* is a "fall guy" or "patsy." *"Myrmidon"* is a term often applied ironically to the henchmen of the law. Lastly, the phrase *"clou à clouer"* could evoke the idea of a "madman (or criminal) to be locked up." Artaud's evident sympathy for criminals is not surprising since he too knows what it means to be imprisoned by society.

Other images also attest to Artaud's anxiety that his being is disintegrating. Panic-stricken at the thought that he is being eaten alive, he speaks of his body as if it were no more than a leg of lamb. "Naked at birth and naked at death, this man who has been cooked, strangled, hung, broiled and baptized, shot and imprisoned, starved and guillotined on the SCAFFOLD of existence." (F, 686) And, in the preface to his complete works he asserts that, for his part, the only important issue is that of being. But he cannot conceive of being except as "being-as-meat." Punning on the words *"carnation* (fleshtint)—*incarnation"* he expresses a desire to pierce the body with words:

> With which words introduced knifelike into the enduring carnation,
>   into an incarnation which really dies under the span of the islet of flame cast by a gallows lantern,
>   I mean whose meat gleams, opaque and recalcitrant,

flatulent empty, proliferating useful, appetizing acid,
   with which words could I enter into the grain of this
menacing meat . . .
   Meat to be bled under the hammer,
   to be rooted out with knife blows.

                                                    (I, 9)

The body is also referred to as meat in a number of other passages. In *Artaud le Momo* Artaud concentrates on the two bodily organs which had always preoccupied him most— the tongue and the sexual organ.

> This tongue between four gums,
>
> This meat between two knees,
> This piece of hole
> for madmen.
>   (Momo, 12)

In general, "meat" is associated with the soft fleshiness and the animality of the body. Bones, on the other hand, represent the purity and hardness which Artaud longed to attain.

> To exist all you have to do is let yourself be,
> but to live,
> you must be someone,
> to be someone
> you must have a BONE,
> not be afraid to show the bone,
> and to lose the meat on the way.
>
> Man has always preferred meat
> to the world of bones.
>   (JD, 20)

Artaud's repeated references to his body as meat indicate not only his disgust with corporeality, but his fear that he will be eaten alive until nothing will remain of his being. This paranoiac obsession is expressed in a variety of ways.

Sometimes he is seized with a dread that evil spirits are preying upon his mind. "For if there is something which tells lies it is really what we call consciousness / which lives for nothing other than to be rotted and baffled by the beasts of the evil spirit."[10] Most of his images, however, are far more concrete and physical. In *Artaud le Momo,* for example, he is set upon by parasitic beings.

> raped, shaved, completely sucked up
> by all the insolent rabble
> by all those fairies stuffed with shit
> who had no other grub
> to live
> than to eat
> Artaud
> Momo
>
>   (Momo, 16)

He lives in horror of the day when the parasites who live off him will consume all his being and thereby kill him. These evil spirits and bloodsucking parasites are akin to the ghouls and vampires which haunt the pages of the gothic novels so dear to the Surrealists. All the misfortunes that beset Artaud are attributed to these invisible creatures; ghouls attack him when he sleeps and cause his nightmares. "A nightmare is never an accident, but an evil brought upon us by a whore, by the mouth of a ghoulish whore who finds us too rich in life, and who sucks upon us with precision to create interferences in our thoughts and catastrophic voids in the passage of the breath of our sleeping body." (CE, 6) Artaud is convinced that his sense of self-alienation is also due to the action of these ghouls, for they attempt to divide him in two so that he will be eternally estranged from himself. He even holds these parasitic evil spirits responsible for his own lack of masculinity: he has no doubt that they maintain their

virility by nourishing themselves on his, Antonin Artaud's,
sexual and anal parts.

> Rubbing of their laden balls,
> on the canal of their anus
> held and fondled well
> in order to suck life from me.
>
> (Momo, 48)

In this passage Artaud apparently equates loss of virility with
the loss of life itself.

Chameleonlike, these parasitic beings which haunt Artaud assume a variety of forms and shapes. Often they appear as loathsome insects and beasts drawn by the sight of
the poet's weak and defenseless body.

> the world of invertebrate larvas
> which sends forth the endless night of
> useless insects:
> > lice,
> > fleas,
> > bedbugs,
> > mosquitoes,
> > spiders,
> is created only
> because the everyday body
> has lost its hunger
> its original cohesion
>
> (84, 129–130)

Not infrequently, the supreme parasite is God himself. God,
who has robbed us of the flame of life, is not only Artaud's
enemy but the foe of all mankind.

> tear of larva
> larva of tear
> of this so-called

langhate [*sic*] of life
where god insisted on seeing the element of life
that he grasped in passing
as he might grasp some flaming mussel or oyster
(EV, 128–129)

The horror Artaud experiences when he contemplates the loss of his being is frequently expressed by metaphors involving holes. A passage in which the sexual organ is so referred to, "this piece of hole for madmen," has already been mentioned in another context. Holes, or voids, represent the non-being, the nothingness, the utter disintegration that terrified Artaud. And, in its ultimate form, such disintegration is death. Artaud has a clear vision of himself as a lifeless hole:

The old Artaud
is buried
in the hole of the fireplace . . .

He is this hole without a frame
that life wanted to frame
(Momo, 17)

(*Le vieil Artaud*
est enterré
dans le trou de la cheminée . . .
Il est ce trou sans cadre
que la vie voulut encadrer)

(Artaud is punning on the word *"encadrer"* [to frame], whose slang meaning is "to attack and strike in the face.") Even the parasitic beings which attack him, and steal his being, come from holes and emptiness. They are forced to seek nourishment from living people, since they are themselves devoid of being. These parasites

are born without cessation,
from each other,

from the holes of the air,
from the roaming vacuities of space.

(84, 99)

The holes which occupy Artaud most are those constituting the body's orifices. The Freudian overtones which this
suggests are rendered more explicit by Artaud's fear that man
will lose his being through these orifices and consequently
die. *"Le visage humain"* ("The Human Face") describes the
cavities and holes on the face of man.

the human face
such as it is, still seeking
itself with two eyes a
nose a mouth
and the two auricular
cavities
which correspond to the holes
of the eye sockets like
the four openings
of the cave of
impending death.[11]

Artaud's dread of bodily orifices is but another aspect of
his lifelong hatred of all the animal functions and instinctual drives within him. As always, chief among the instincts
he despises is sexuality, which, he now declares, is at the root
of all our other animal functions.

for hunger, appetite, taste, the need for food
stem solely from this muscle of infamous pleasure
with which man made love.

(EV, 130)

Artaud's desire to escape from his animal functions leads
him to create his own Rousseauistic paradise. He declares
that in the past man had no instincts and lived in a state of

plantlike purity. This idyllic epoch must have occurred quite recently for he can even remember when he himself was free of all animality:

> I was an old tree with grooves
> which didn't eat
> didn't drink
> didn't breathe
> and all the crappers of spermy shit
> and of shitty mucus
> wormed themselves into me
>
> surrounding my slightest filaments
> and making a sub-elemental life for themselves
> of tomblike depths
> a secret double of life
> which they wanted to bring to life to replace mine
>
> (EV, 129)

The image of a tree—a symbol of purity—is also found in a letter-poem Artaud wrote to his friend Pierre Loeb. This time, however, the tree, made of man's free will, reflects Artaud's desire to dominate himself and others. Deeply disturbed by his own weakness and impotence, Artaud dreams nostalgically of a time when man possessed an all-powerful will:

> The time when man was a tree without organs or functions,
> but of will
> and a walking tree of will
> shall return.
>
> (PL, 481)

Artaud's revulsion at man's present degradation is heightened by his conviction that man should have refused to accept all loathsome bodily functions. He could have accomplished this by simply rejecting life itself. But, coward that he was, man allowed himself to become encumbered with bestial instincts.

> Where you smell shit
> you smell human existence.
> Man could very well not have shit,
> not have opened his anal pocket,
> but he chose to shit
> just as he could have chosen to live
> instead of consenting to a living death.
>
> (JD, 19)

Artaud's fear of external hostile forces leads him to denounce with particular relish all those bodily functions—such as eating and copulating—which involve other people or things. If need be, he would destroy all the organs which traffic with the outside world.

> You must be chaste in order to know how not to eat
> To open your mouth is to expose yourself to the miasmas
> Therefore, no mouth!
> No mouth!
> no tongue
> no teeth . . .
>
> (84, 102)

He would especially like to eliminate the tongue, an organ that is doubly threatening. Not only does it reach for food from the outside; it is also the instrument whereby we communicate our thoughts to others.

> Because you have let the tongue hand out from organisms
> it was necessary to cut off the tongue
> from these organisms
> at the exit of the body's tunnels.
>
> (84, 127)

It is conceivable, also, that Artaud wants to cut off his tongue in order to effect a symbolic castration. This may appear to be a strained interpretation, inasmuch as he had always longed to be strong and masculine. But, it must be remembered that he also longed for sexual purity. And, in the few years preceding his death, hatred of sexuality far outweighed any anxiety he may have had about his virility. Again and again Artaud denies that man is essentially a sexual being.

> a true man has no sex
> he is not aware of this hideous thing
> and this stupefying sin
> instead he has attained the perfection
> that man
> by definition
> will never know
>
> (84, 112)

Contradicting all that he had said earlier about primordial sexual conflicts, he now asserts that in the beginning there was no differentiation between the sexes.

More than any other aspect of sexuality, it is sodomy that arouses Artaud's wrath. Undoubtedly, this preoccupation with the anus was at least partially due to the fact that Artaud was suffering from a rectal disease. However, it is highly probable that this attitude also stems from Artaud's doubts concerning his virility, and his fear that the female within him would render him an easy sexual prey. This same anxiety was at the root of his interest in weak, emasculated and homosexual men, such as Uccello, Abelard, and Heliogabalus. Artaud was not as fortunate as the last of these, the pederast–king who succeeded in reconciling the male and female elements within himself. As the years passed, Artaud's inner sexual tension grew more acute. In 1946 he confessed to a friend that even before birth he had wondered whether he was to be man or woman. Although he goes on to assure his friend that he did in fact become a man, his assurance lacks conviction. "Will I go to the mother or will I stay the father . . . ? You must believe that I must have chosen to be the father for eternity, since I have been a man for fifty years now and I don't see how that can change."[12]

Hatred of the body, with its animal functions and instincts, is far more than a simple desire for purity; in rejecting the body Artaud is refusing to accept the human condition with all its limitations. Time and again he tells us that he is not part of mankind. To prove to us that he is really different he repeatedly asserts that, unlike ordinary mortals, he was not born of a mother and a father. This declaration is doubly significant. If he had no parents, his birth could not have resulted from sexual intercourse. Secondly, if he has not been created like other men, he is not subject to the laws which govern humanity—the laws of life and death.

Birth is associated with all that is repulsive and loathsome. In *Ci-gît,* Artaud describes a warrior who chooses death rather than go through his mother's organs in the process of birth. He (the warrior)

> did not want to go through
> the periplus of the serpent
> that bites its tail from up front
> while papa-mama
> makes his behind all bloody

The parents, derogatively called "papa-mama," punish the warrior (a disguised Artaud) because he does not accede to their demand that he be born. An even more brutal image depicts his parents in the act of copulating on his diseased body, in an attempt to create a child. The mother and father could scarcely be more repellent:

she, 35 years
he, 45, already ripe,
are making the kid in the water of nard,
on all the wounds of Artaud's pain,
at the spot where the pain,
blood, musk, nard, urine, feces-farts [*vèces*], snot,
ecchymosis, scabs,
tumors,
pharyngitis, meningitis
of Artaud
gives the most priclish [*chatouné*] kid[13]

(*"Vèces"* has been translated as "feces-farts" since it suggests "feces" and also *"vesse,"* which means "fart." Similarly, *"chatouné"* brings to mind *"chatouiller"* [to tickle] and *"chatonné"* [sexually excited], and hence, "priclish.") The realization that a child is created by a "mother who didn't ask him anything" horrifies Artaud. He cannot accept the fact that children are forced into birth, without their consent or desire, because of the "obscene" wishes of parents.

His repeated insistence that he was not born like other men reflects not only Artaud's abhorrence of sex but also an intense desire to create himself. He wants to be alone responsible for his existence. Intransigently he declares, "I come from myself / truly from me," and tells us that he was the first man on earth:

> in the filth
> of a paradise
> in which the first fool on earth
> was not the father nor the mother
> who remade you in this cave
>   but
>   ME
> screwed down in my madness.
>   (Momo, 16)

The mention of paradise suggests that even God had nothing
to do with the creation of Antonin Artaud. The notion of
divine creation is rejected even more explicitly in *Ci-gît* in
which Artaud mocks the concept of the Holy Trinity.

> I, Antonin Artaud, I am my son,
>   my father, my mother
>   and myself.

Not content to declare that he owes nothing to God, Artaud cannot resist the temptation to proselytize: He who does
not reject the idea of a God-creator is a coward. "I hate
and denounce as a coward every being who consents to having been made and does not want to be remade / That is,
all those who accept the idea of a god-creator at the origin
of their being and their thought." (JL, 280) By creating himself, he can become the man he longs to be—dominant, hard
and pure—and do away with the Artaud who is at the mercy
of everyone and everything.

> I only believe in one thing
> that my deepest strength will not restore me
> but will *establish me*
>   *myself*
>   Antonin Artaud
> such that I know, *feel* and desire myself
> > (LS, 138)

The need for power leads Artaud to make ever greater demands: He would like to control not only himself, but
everything else in the universe. Only in this way will his
fear of the exterior world and of his own weakness be finally
assuaged.

> I know only one *hazy* thing
> and I know it very hazily
> and that is that

> *I*
> *Antonin Artaud*
> I am the master of things
> and it's *I*
> who's made them and makes them . . .
> but there is another thing I know
> not hazily but clearly
> and that is that things
>   and *beings*
> inevitably obey the commandment of my breath
>   (LS, 136–137)

Since his will is shaken at the sign of the slightest resistance, he feels secure only if he is the absolute, unquestioned master of all things.

His wish to create other beings and things is matched by his desire to keep his own being intact in the process. In this respect, even the process of literary creation is fraught with danger:

> I am this primitive, unsatisfied
> with the inexpiable horror of
> things. I do not want to reproduce
> myself in things, but I
> want things to be produced
> through me. I do not want an
> idea of myself in my poem, and
> I do not want to see myself in it.[14]

Since Artaud attributes concrete reality to words, he does not distinguish between the "idea" of being and being itself. Thus, if he saw an "idea" of himself in his poems it would mean that he had lost some portion of his own existence. Consequently, he risks his very life by writing; yet, without his poems he would be nothing.

> We are 50 poems,
> the rest isn't us but the nothingness which clothes us,

laughs at us first,
and then lives off us.

(PL, 483)

Artaud's need to create and govern himself has still another important facet. If he owes his life to others, then
everything that happens to him is pure accident. He might
have been born fifty years previously, or not at all. The
thought that everything is created and lives by accident and
chance fills Artaud with horror. Nothing would reassure him
more than the certitude that the universe is governed by
a divine plan. If there were such a plan, Artaud would be
relieved of all responsibility for his own existence. But, as
things stand, he is not strong enough to be his own master,
nor is he under the sway of an all-encompassing cosmic order.
Knowing that his life depends upon mere chance, he bitterly
reproaches God for this fortuitousness. Time was when man
could control and order the world:

> the magical life of man has fallen,
> man has fallen from his magnetic rock,
> and the inspiration which was the base
> has become chance, accident.

(PL, 484)

Man can return to his former happy state, says Artaud, only
if he can purify life of all that is unnecessary. Playing on the
expression "*sans condition,*" which could mean either "un
conditioned" or "lacking in status (or station)," Artaud exhorts us to get rid of

> The rats of the unconditioned
> Who have never felt
>> That
>> The non-form
>> The outside-of-place

of the unconditioned anger
called the without-state . . .

are not worth the peelings
from the cunt of a dead whore
(Momo, 30–31)

(*Des rats de l'inconditionné*
Qui n'ont jamais senti
Que

La non-forme

Le hors-lieu
de la rogne sans condition
appelée le sans condition . . .

ne valent pas les desquamations
du con d'une moniche morte)

(The word *"moniche,"* translated here as "whore," appears to have been created by Artaud. *"Mouniche,"* however, is slang for the female sex, while *"momiche"* is the diminutive for a woman or a prostitute.) Although man has been cast out of a better world, all can still be set right if Artaud assumes the role of God. Convinced that he will be able to abolish the reign of Accident and Chance, he aspires to be a kind of Demiurge. In one poem he asserts that he is God. The being we call God—who is nothing more than a clever vampire—projected himself into Artaud's body and continues to exist at the price of Artaud's life. This so-called God

found nothing better
in order *to be*
than to be born at the price of
my assassination
(84, 109)

Even the possession of godlike powers could not satisfy Artaud for what he really seeks is a transformation of life itself. Utterly disillusioned with the mind and soul of man,

Artaud now transfers his former spiritual and mystical desires onto the body. Even as he attributes all loathsome bodily functions to the *mind,* he demands that the *body* be completely purified and transformed. Whereas he had formerly sought to purify his mind and soul by liberating them from their material prisons, he now asks that the body itself achieve absolute purity. Far from having disappeared, his former gnostic desire to live in a world free of matter and corporeality has grown stronger than ever before.

> Furthermore man will be what I want
> a pure body
> and not
> pure spirit

> (84, 112)

Man has not yet realized his full possibilities because he has been barred from "true" life by hostile and calculating creatures.

> The human body is an electric battery
> whose discharges have been castrated and repressed
>
> whose abilities and tones
> have been oriented toward sexual life

> (84, 122)

To achieve purity, man must first rid himself of all his organs. Jacques Derrida observes that Artaud wanted to discard organs because of their association with the bodily orifices through which he loses his being. "The organ always functions as an opening. The reconstruction and the reestablishment of my flesh depends upon the closing in of the body upon itself and the reduction of its organic structure."[15] Our organs, says Artaud, have been grafted onto us by a demonic God bent on preventing man from attaining the desired state.

> When you give him a body without organs
> then you will deliver him from all his automatic reflexes
> and return him to his true liberty.
>
> (JD, 40)

In addition to the removal of our organs, Artaud would like to eliminate all sensations and physical contact.

> I will be chaste and pure,
> virgin, intact, untouchable. . . .
>
> I hate and denounce as a coward all sensations and all beings.
>
> I hate and denounce the so-called sensations of being.
>
> I am by nature clean and pure.
>
> (JL, 283)

By ridding himself of all sensations, Artaud hopes to sever contact with the outside world and thus insulate himself from external hostile forces. His former belief that he could achieve this invulnerability by becoming hard and virile also remained with him. He continued to associate hardness with purity and inviolability; shortly before his death, he expressed a wish to create a theater in which man would cease to be a "swollen creature" and would become, instead, a "sculptural object." (84, 120)

This reference to the theater indicates that Artaud's new attitude toward the body has influenced his dramatic concepts. No longer does he describe the "theater of cruelty" in terms of metaphysical and cosmic forces. Instead, he pathetically cries out that the theater must enable man to find the purity and health he has so tragically lost. "I have conceived of a theater of cruelty which dances and screams/ in order to topple organs and sweep away germs." (JD, 51) By purifying the body, the theater would allow it to live forever.

The theater is not this scenic display where a myth is
  developed
virtually and symbolically
  but a crucible of fire and true meat where anatomically,
  by trampling bones, limbs and syllables,
      bodies are remade . . .
  The human body dies only because we have forgotten how
    to transform
and change it.[16]

What Artaud demands of a corporeal transformation is not
only purity but immortality itself. Although he had never
before expressed his desire so unequivocally, throughout his
life he had sought to escape from the bonds of the human
condition—through Eastern mysticism, occultism, and Catholicism. Toward the end of his stay at Rodez he was faced
with a difficult dilemma: Having denied the existence of the
soul and spiritual phenomena, how was he to sustain any
hope that man might be immortal? Confronted with this
problem, he reversed once again the roles usually attributed
to the body and to the mind and declared that we could
achieve immortality through our bodies.

A number of other passages reveal the intensity of Artaud's
spiritual longings. Like many believers, Artaud thinks that
we live in a world of appearances. A messianic fervor marks
his conviction that

    we have not yet been born,

    we are not yet in the world,

    there is no world yet,

    things have not yet been made,

    the reason for being has not been found.

        (JL, 283)

With unshakeable faith Artaud tells us that he will shortly leave this false life: "But the sleeper that I am will not fail to awaken/and I think this will happen very soon." (EV, 131)

As in his earliest poems, the very terminology Artaud employs is frequently drawn from mystical literature. For example, he expresses an ardent wish to unite with the sun. All that is human must be discarded if this union is to take place.

> Withdraw the body from what is human
> into the light of nature
> plunge it panting into the gleam of nature
> where it shall finally wed with the sun
> (84, 100)

Finally, one of Artaud's most touching poems expresses his faith that he will soon experience a "miracle," one which will grant him at once inner peace and immortality.

> It is not possible that in the end the miracle won't burst forth
> I have been so tortured. . . .
> I have tried so hard to have a clean body.
> (84, 135)

Antonin Artaud's thirst for the godlike power to govern himself and others was paralleled by the desire to found his own language—one which would be free of all pre-established structures of thought and meaning. This desire stemmed not only from his drive to be creator and master of all things, but also from his lifelong distrust of ordinary language. In the course of the years, he had turned to painting, to gestures, to sounds—all in an effort to find a system of signs to replace the words which constantly betrayed him. By establishing his own language he would accomplish a double aim: Not only would this enable him to assert his complete and utter independence from the exterior world,

but he could also wreak final vengeance upon traitorous
everyday language.

Révolte contre la poésie, a poem written in 1944 while
he was still at Rodez, explains why it is so important to
Artaud that he create a new language. In this, he voices his
fear that he has no control over his words, and that a vague
unconscious has designated him to write certain poems. Convinced that this unconscious force is attempting to invade his
being, he cries out that he alone must determine what he is
to write:

> I do not
> want words which come from
> god knows what astral libido
> which was completely aware of the
> formations of my own desires.

He is fighting a losing battle, however, for this unconscious
is clever enough to ferret out Artaud's desires and ideas and
dictate them back to him. Consequently, Artaud cannot
prove that what he writes depends upon someone else. Furthermore, since this unconscious force has invaded his very
being, he must rid himself of it (this "astral libido") and
also of his "self" which has been enslaved.

> I do not want to be the poet
> of my poet, of this self who wanted
> to choose me to be a poet, but the
> poet-creator, in revolt against
> the ego and the self.

The words *"moi"* and *"soi"* have been translated respectively
as "ego" and "self." (It seems likely that Artaud uses these
words in the same way as Hindu thinkers, who believe that
the ego is only a transient modification of the transcendent
and permanent principle that is the self.) By ridding him-

self of the "self" and the "ego," Artaud will also free himself of language, which he regards as just one more hostile force.

> It is by rebelling against the
> self and the ego that I rid
> myself of all evil
> incarnations of the Word
> which have never been anything
> else for man than a compromise
> between cowardice and illusion.

As a poet, Artaud is especially vulnerable since he is constantly dealing with words, which possess the power to destroy him. With every poem he risks his life.

> There is in the forms of
> the human Word I don't know what
> process of greed, what
> self-devouring greed whereby the
> poet, attaching himself to the object,
> sees himself eaten by it.

Artaud's anguish is partly sexual in nature for he is afraid that he will be raped by his own creation. And he has neither the strength nor the virility to defend himself.

> To give your
> self to your poem is also
> to risk being violated by it.
> And if I am Virgin for my
> poem, it should stay virgin
> for me.

In spite of Artaud's repeated assertions that he wants to create his own language, he rarely explains how he hopes to accomplish this aim. The only aspect of language which he discusses at any length involves the *sound* of words. While at Rodez he claimed to have written a book (which he later declared lost) entitled *Letura d'Eprahi Talli Tetr Frendi Photia O Fotre Indi*. This book, Artaud claimed, was written in a universal language of sounds which could be understood by people of every nationality. Even if Artaud did write this book (and that seems highly unlikely), the title alone indicates that his invented "universal" language was greatly indebted to the French vocabulary.

Artaud's preoccupation with sounds is consistent with his aim to create a language which could affect men physically rather than intellectually. He regards poetry, including his own, as a failure if it does not sway the bodies of men. "If I am a poet or an actor it is not in order to write or declaim a poem . . . or to be applauded, but to feel the bodies of men and women—yes, *bodies*—tremble and turn in unison with mine." (R, 19) Convinced that the *sound* of words can affect our bodies, he declares that all poetry must be given voice. "All poems have been written first and foremost to be heard and to be concretized by spoken voices . . . an authentic poem only makes sense away from the printed or written page."[17]

While the sound of words plays an extremely important role in Artaud's later poetry, it is highly doubtful that these poems accomplish the aims Artaud himself had in mind. He wanted to create a *new* language which would both coincide with the author's being and affect the listener in a physical way. Even Artaud's most fervent admirers could scarcely maintain that he was successful in these objectives. His language is not new and, far from having a physical effect, the poems demand all the resources of the reader's intellectual and mental ingenuity. Artaud's use of word sounds brings to mind James Joyce and Lewis Carroll. Although both Joyce and Carroll indulge in innumerable verbal tricks and games involving the sound of words, neither of them could be said to have invented a new language. When Joyce tells us, at the beginning of *Finnegans Wake,* that "Sir Tristram, violer d'amores, fr'over the short sea, had passencore rearrived from North Armorica on this side the scraggy isthmus of Europe Minor to Wielderfight his penisolate war," all the words he "creates" suggest existing words. Similarly, Carroll's "Jabberwocky," which begins " 'Twas brillig, and the slithy toves/ Did gyre and gimble in the wabe," only makes sense because the invented words evoke ones we already know: lithe and slim (slithy), gyroscope (gyre), gambol and nimble (gimble), and wave (wabe).

But Artaud does not appear to use these puns, neologisms, and word games merely to demonstrate the importance of sound. One has the impression that he deliberately wants to make his poems obscure so that he will not expose himself to his enemies. Through the intricacy of the language he uses, he is attempting to defend himself against the hostile forces threatening him. Further, Artaud had always reacted against the fixed and arbitrary nature of words. By using puns and playing with words, he is in effect demonstrating that any given word or phrase has more than one meaning or level of interpretation. His scorn for the "characteristic rigidity" of words leads him to twist ordinary language almost beyond recognition.

While countless scholars have played intellectual games with Joyce for many years now, the exegesis of Artaud's work is just beginning. But whereas Joyce might have been amused by all the mental activity devoted to his work, Artaud, were he now alive, would have reacted in horror. Throughout his life he had declared war on intellectual endeavors that were removed from what he considered the real problems of existence. It is not hard to imagine how Artaud would feel if he knew that a host of literary scholars were dissecting his poems. It is a supreme paradox that the man who wished

to write only for "illiterates" should have produced a body
of work which, as of today, is accessible only to scholars and,
as he himself would say, "initiates."

However difficult Artaud's poems may be, many readers
consider them to be the finest portion of his work. Although
Artaud could never eliminate traditional language, nor make
language coincide with being, he, like other important contemporary writers, did push language to a breaking point.
Had he gone further, had he wrenched language out of its
traditional patterns any more than he did, any communication would have been impossible. As it is, many passages in
his later poems are partially, if not totally, incomprehensible.
Rather than generalize further, it is well to turn to the poems
themselves, to Artaud's language of sounds.

Word games and puns abound whenever Artaud gives
vent to his hatred of sexuality and parents. This is well illustrated in a passage taken from *"Centre mère et patron
minet,"* a poem constituting one section of *Artaud le Momo:*

> *et il fallut ventre à ventre cogner*
> *chaque mère qui voulait pénétrer*
>
> chatte mitte en patron-minet
>
> *dans l'exsangue tube insurgé*
> *comme au centre*
> *de la panaceé:*
> chatte-mite et patron minet
> *sont les deux vocables salauds*
> que père et mère ont
>   inventés
>
> *pour jouir de lui au plus gros.*
>   (Momo, 24–25)

> (And you had to beat, belly against
> belly, each mother who wanted to penetrate
>
> *pussy prison into owner-pussy*

in the rebellious bloodless tube
as in the center
of the panacea:
pussy-prison and owner pussy
are the two filthy words
that mother and father have
invented

to enjoy him as much as possible.)

The play of words in this passage is complex. *"Chatte"* and *"minet"* both mean "cat," but they are also slang for the female sex (the "pussy"), and can even be applied to homosexuals. The term *"chattemite"* refers to a person who is sweet and gentle in appearance only. The word *"mite"* denotes the insect, as it does in English, but it is also slang for "prison." So, Artaud would seem to be associating the female sex *(chatte mitte)* with the idea of imprisonment and simulated sweetness. *"Patron"* is commonly used to designate a male owner or proprietor. Assuming that *"minet"* is used here to denote an effeminate man, *"patron minet"* evokes the image of an effeminate male (or male organ). (Although *"patron minet"* also calls to mind *"Potron minet,"* which means "early morning," it can scarcely have that meaning here.) The supposition that *"patron minet"* and *"chatte nitte"* refer, respectively, to the male and female organs is supported by the title of the passage, since *"patron minet"* suggests a weak male while *"centre mère"* makes one think of a strong female. In this case, the "bloodless tube" would obviously be a reference to the vagina. So, once again, Artaud is revealing his fear that he will be emasculated by a virile female. He also fears that the *"chatte mitte"* and the *"patron minet,"* the two unspeakable organs, are going to "enjoy" the child they create, here none other than Artaud himself. The title of another poem, *"Centre pitere et potron chier,"* appears related to *"Centre mère et patron minet."*

Since *"potron minet"* means "early morning," it is reasonable to assume that *"potron chier"* means *"chier tous les
matins"* (to shit every morning). *"Centre pitere"* suggests
both *"centre père"* and *"piteux"* (pitiful), hence "pitiful
father." Many of the words in these poems seem to have
been chosen because, like the words for mother and father
(mère and *père),* they begin with m and p. This device is
also found in a passage taken from *Ci-gît* in which Artaud
describes parents thus:

> *Pitre affreux de père mimire,*
> *Immonde pitri parasite, dans creux*
> *   mamiche retiré du feul*

> (Frightful clown of papa mimicsee,
> Filthy clowi parasite, in the hollow
>   mamass torn from the fire!)

Verbal tricks are often employed to attack Christianity
as well as sexuality and parenthood. In one poem Artaud
tells us that Jesus' body *"s'est a pelait,"* which could either
imply *"s'est appelé* (is named) or *"a pelé"* (pealed). Jesus,

> *qui ne fut crucifié qu'en esprit*
> *pendant que son corps*
> *s'est a pelait*
>
> (84, 120)

> (who was crucified only in spirit
> while his body
> was pealed)

Throughout *Ci-gît* Artaud plays with the name "Jesus
Christ," converting it into "ji cri" and "jiji-cricri." Although
it may not be wholly clear at the beginning of the poem that
these words refer to Christ, as the poem progresses any
doubts we may have are dispelled.

What does that mean?
That means that papa-mama will stop buggering
                    the innate pederast
the filthy pricker of christian
                orgies
interloper between ji and cri
contracted into jiji-cricri

Even without realizing that jiji-cricri means Jesus Christ, it is
clear that the passage involves sex and creation, two of Artaud's principal obsessions. The "papa-mama" will no longer
be able to indulge in its usual sexual practices. Although
"papa-mama" is usually a reference to parents, in this context it appears to mean God-the-creator (or God and Mary),
since the line that follows speaks of "christian orgies." The
knowledge that "jiji-cricri" is Christ, however, enriches this
passage. For then we see that Jesus Himself is the "innate
pederast" who no longer has anything to fear from an aggressive God. So does Artaud endow Jesus with his own fear
that he will be sexually victimized and sodomized. And the
fact that Jesus' name suggests *"cri"* (scream) reveals the violence which Artaud associates with sex and Christianity.

The second passage, in which "ji" and "cri" reappear, is
even more complex than the preceding one. Toward the
middle of *Ci-gît,* Artaud tells us that:

It is thus that they
tore from me
papa and mamma
and the frying of ji in
Cri
out of the sex (the center)
of the great strangulation
whence was torn this cross
                    ing of the bier

(dead)

and of the matter
which gave life
to Jizo-cri
when from the dung of
    my dead *self*
        was torn
the blood
    which guilds
        all stolen life
        outside.

Here Artaud's thirst for the power of creation comes to the
fore. Not only does he assert that he gave birth to his parents, but he maintains that the reign of God (the absolute
creator) and Jesus Christ will soon come to an end. Horrified, as always, at the thought of copulation, he associates
sexuality with death. Coffins and decaying matter spring
forth from our sexual parts, the "center of strangulation."
Next, he expresses his hatred of Christ by telling us that
Jesus was born from matter, and that the cross itself was
"torn" from sexuality. Finally, the last lines in this passage testify to his fear that parasitic beings will kill him in
order to nourish themselves on his dead body and even
on his excrement.

    The last mention of "Jizo-cri" occurs toward the end of
the poem. Artaud is apparently convinced that Christ is an
impostor and that he, Antonin Artaud, is truly Jesus Christ.

    don't you see that the fake son-in-law
    is Jizi-cri,
    already known in Mexico
    long before his flight to Jerusalem on a donkey
    and the crucifixion of Artaud at Golgotha

Artaud's assertion that Jesus Christ was first known in Mexico probably stems from the fact that the ancient Mexican

religion worshiped a figure similar to Christ. His own persecution complex moves him to identify with Christ, the supreme victim. In the course of the poem, it gradually becomes clear that "jiji-cricri" is a focal point around which
converge the various themes of sex, religion, and creation.

The intensity of Artaud's obsession with man's animal
instincts can be gauged by the number of verbal tricks he
devotes to them. Certain parts of the body—the tongue, the
anus, and the sexual organs—preoccupied him more than
others. He often puns, for example, on the word for tongue
(la langue), which in French as in English, denotes the ana-
tomical member as well as language in general. In *"Coleridge
le traître,"* the poet is disturbed by both these aspects of
"tongue": "The English tongue had played on Samuel Tay-
lor Coleridge's open, truthful, intrinsic heart . . . one of
these dirty tricks which tongues of meat can never refrain
themselves from playing on the hearts of budding poets."
(SR, 22)

In many of Artaud's last poems anal functions claim more
puns and word games than the tongue. This is certainly true
of a short poem entitled *"Histoire du Popocatepel."*

> *Quand je pense homme, je pense*
> *patate, popo, caca, tete* [sic]*, papa,*
> *et à l'l de la petite haleine qui en sort pour ranimer ça.*
> *Patate, nécessité du pot d'être, qui peut-être aura sa potée.*
> *Et après patate, caca, souffle du double vé cé s'il vous*
> *plaît des cachots de nécessité.*
>
> (F, 686)

(When I think man, I think of
idiot, popo, caca, head, papa,
and of the wing of the little breath which is exhaled to
    animate that.
Idiot, necessity of the pot of being, which *perhaps* will
    have its potful.

And after idiot, caca, breath of the double-you-sea if you
please these dungeons of necessity.)

The meaning of this passage emerges only after unraveling
some intricate puns and word games. In slang *"pot"* refers
to the anus. *"Popo,"* which sounds like *"pot-pot,"* is a child's
word for *caca*. So, in the second line Artaud is associating
man's excrement *(popo-caca)* with the concepts of things he
despises, such as intellectuality *(tete-head)* and parenthood
(papa). The "little breath" in the following line apparently
refers to the emission of bodily gas, for its *"l'l,"* which sounds
the same as *"l'aile,"* or "wing," helps it to fly. Heaping one
scatological pun upon another, Artaud then proceeds to play
with the word *"pot"*: The phrase *"nécessité du pot d'être"*
takes cognizance of the necessity for the anal function. At
the same time, *"pot d'être"* is similar in sound to *"peut-être"*
(perhaps). In light of all this, the word *"potée"* is obviously
a reference to man's excrement. Finally, when man needs to
eliminate he makes use of the *"double vé cé,"* which, if
sounded out, is a w.c., or a "dungeon of necessity."

Some of Artaud's most successful puns and word games involve words possessing both a spiritual and a pornographic
or scatological meaning. He uses linguistic games to mock
the spiritual concepts which he was vehemently rejecting at
the end of his life. One such pun, found in the *Lettres de
Rodez* (p. 21), speaks of the soul in terms usually reserved
for anal functions: 'I'm touching bottom,' says the man regarding life, to indicate that he is at the bottom of his death,
that the silver surface of his soul is a pierced abyss for him."
*(Je suis à cul, dit l'homme de la vie pour signifier qu'il est
au fond de sa morte, que le tain du miroir de son âme est
un gouffre percé pour lui.)* The term *"gouffre percé"* seems
meaningless, but it does bring to mind the expression *"chaise
percée,"* which denotes a "pierced chair," formerly used by

man for excremental functions. By speaking of the soul so, Artaud reduces it to the level of matter, of dung. The soul is similarly derided in *Pour en finir avec le jugement de dieu;* Artaud combines the word for soul with other words describing sexual practices.

> *Ils dansent la danse de la friction infâme*
> *de la futame avec lâ* [sic] *fame et*
> *de l'union de ron et saun.*

> (JD, 47–48)

> (They dance the dance of the vile rubbing
> of the fucame with the dame and
> of the union of ron and saun.)

Although the meaning of *"ron"* and *"saun"* is not clear, *"futame"* is certainly a combination of *"foutre"* (to fuck) and *"âme"* (soul), while *"fame"* sounds exactly the same as *"femme"* (woman).

Many of the puns involving spiritual concepts use words drawn from diverse religious sects and mystical doctrines—a fact which often renders Artaud's games esoteric. A favorite word is "ka," which in the ancient Egyptian religion signified the immaterial double of man's body. In the letter from Rodez mentioned above, Artaud asserts, "The breath of the bones has a center and this center is the pit Kah-Kah, Kah the corporeal breath of shit, which is the opium of eternal afterlife." *(Le souffle des ossements a un centre et ce centre est le gouffre Kah-Kah, Kah le souffle corporel de la merde, qui est l'opium d'éternelle survie.)* By transforming the word "ka" into "Kah-Kah," or *"caca,"* Artaud is mocking the idea that man's body has a spiritual double; he implies that everything can be reduced to matter, and ultimately to *"caca."* Other examples of puns involving the "ka" are found in the poem *"Fragmentations"* (p. 679), in which Artaud states that "insulin is Ka without shit, shit without making caca" (*l'insuline c'est du Ka sans merde, de la merde sans faire caca*). Farther on in the poem (p. 684), he speaks to us of imaginary daughters of his; although they have been dead for a long time, he can see their corpses which, "beyond the distress of their limbs [of limbo] are waiting, before coming to me, for me to finish marrying my Ka Ka" (*qui par delà la détresse des limbes, attendent pour venir à moi que j'ai fini d'épouser mon Ka Ka*). Here there is a double pun concerning the material and the spiritual. *"Limbes"* refers to both limbo and the limbs of the body; either meaning makes sense in this context. Then, there is the inevitable pun on "Ka-*caca*." By declaring that he will marry his "Ka Ka," Artaud suggests that, upon his death, he will merge with his spiritual double. In this case, however, the spiritual double is made of excrement.

Next to "ka" the esoteric word most frequently mentioned by Artaud is "Aum" (sometimes spelled "Om"). A sacred word in the Hindu religion, Aum symbolizes the Absolute. True believers seek to unite with this Absolute and thereby lose all sense of their individual selves. As a holy exclamation Aum is placed at the beginning and at the end of every recital of the Vedas. In *"Là où j'en suis"* the word "Aum" is found in a passage which explores the nature of the relationship between the body and the mind. Unable to accept its existence, Artaud describes his body so:

> C'est cet
>   a-um
>   cet ah-na
>   cet a ha
>   cet ha mah
>   cet ah-mah
> qui n'est pas mā

> *mais lā-h.*
>
>   (LS, 133)
>   (It's this
>   a-um
>   this ah-na
>   this a ha
>   this ha mah
>   this ah-mah
>   which is not ma
>   but la-h)

If we take *"mā"* and *"lā-h"* to mean, respectively, *"moi"* (me) and *"là"* (there), Artaud is apparently claiming that his body does not really belong to him *(qui n'est pas mā)* but belongs elsewhere *(mais lā-h).*

Om lends itself to puns even more easily than Aum. Witness the following passage from *Ci-gît:*

> *om-let cadran*
>   [ceci chuchoté]
>
> *vous ne saviez pas ça*
> *que l'état*
>   OEUF
>   *était l'état*
> *anti-artaud*
> *par excellence*
> *et que pour empoisonner artaud*
> *il n'y a rien*
> *de tel que de battre*
> *une bonne omelette*
>
> (om-let face
>   *(whisper this)*
>
> didn't you know
> that the state of
>   *EGG*

                  was the anti-artaud
           state
           par excellence
           and that for poisoning artaud
           there's nothing
           like beating up
           a good omelet)

The association of the egg with fertility and creation would explain why Artaud regards it with hostility.

"*Om-let*" is not the only pun that Artaud creates with Om. In one section of "*Suppôts et supplications*" ("Demons and Death"), Artaud uses Om to mean "*homme*" (man).

> *chacun des corps du collogame*
> *aura l'esprit universel,*
> *où en gîte le per-isprit,*
> *esprit passe-partout et pour tout,*
> *des couilles torses de mon trou*
> *des trouilles de mon trou du cou*
> *aux couves de mon tour de con,*
> *love à persil de ma grumelle*
> *au montil de ma mante umelle*
> *que les rômes hissèrent pet*
> *un jour que l'om voulut om pisser*[18]

> (each of the bodies of the collogame
> will have the universal spirit,
> wherein lies the perisprit,
> spirit which goes everywhere and for everyone,
> twisted balls of my hole
> fears of my neck-hole
> in the house of my cunt tower
> love at the curb of my whormelle
> at the sex of my mante umelle
> that the whores farted
> one day that man wanted man to piss)

In this complex passage *"om"* is preceded by other puns and words, many of which are indecipherable. The word *"collogame"* probably comes from *"coller,"* which could mean "to make love." Literally, *"perisprit"* denotes a fluid that is said to unite the body and the mind, but it also suggests *"père-esprit,"* which could be a reference to God. *"Trouilles,"* a few lines later, means "fear" in slang but also suggests two other key words in the passage: *"trou"* (hole) and *"couilles"* (balls). The expression *"tour de con"* could mean a number of things: either "cunt trick," "cunt tower" or, if *"con"* is used figuratively, "stupid trick." While the word *"grumelle"* does not exist, a *"grue"* is an easy woman, and *"persil"* in slang refers to solicitation by prostitutes. In this context, it is reasonable to conclude that *"love"* retains its English meaning. The last three lines of the poem contain the most obscure words of all, although the fact that Artaud is obviously concerned with sex does provide some clues. For example, it is highly likely that Artaud had the words *"monte"* (an encounter with a prostitute) or *"mons Veneris"* (female sex) in mind when he created *"montil."* *"Mante"* usually denotes a praying mantis—an insect which might well have had a special interest for Artaud because the female of the species devours the male.

Thus far, no mention has been made of the incantatory passages strewn throughout Artaud's later poems. Most of his critics believe that these passages reflect the importance he placed upon sounds. Eric Sellin, a critic who has devoted a book to Artaud's theatrical ideas, concludes an analysis of one incantatory passage with the observation that "certain words in these representative texts resemble real words (papa, mama, dama, repara, ortura, kurbura, kenya, ante) and others may be explained in terms of the Artaud mythos (eme, kurbata, koma, pesti and pestantum), but they are essentially meaningless utterances, objectified word sounds."[19] Although

Artaud's incantations are undeniably related to his preoccupation with sound, it seems highly probable that they are motivated by something more fundamental. Earlier, Artaud had been attracted to mythical thought in part because it did not distinguish between the reality of words and the things they designated. His tendency to believe in the "reality" of words was no doubt encouraged by his readings in Jewish mysticism. In the Cabala, letters and words constitute the base of all creation since they are considered to be an emanation from God. Divine language is the substance of reality. "The uniting bond in creation are the twenty-two letters of the Hebrew alphabet and the first ten numbers (expressed by the first ten letters). These two types of signs are called the thirty-two ways of wisdom upon which God has founded His name. They are identified with thought rendered visible, and they are superior to bodies and substances."[20] The role the Cabalists ascribed to letters and numbers led to a complicated letter-magic which was used to discover hidden meanings in the letters and words of the Hebrew Bible. Numbers were equated with letters, so that connections between words could be discovered through a calculation of their numerical values, and certain letters could be substituted for others. "Any word may yield a hidden meaning by its anagram. In writing the twenty-two letters of the Hebrew alphabet in a special order and in two lines, the letters above and below placed in relationship may substitute for each other."[21] Although Artaud did not employ the letter and number magic established by the Cabalists with any uniformity, a number of his word games do recall the Cabalistic use of letter permutations and combinations, particularly in the interchange of one letter for another.

Artaud's conviction that language is "real" is obviously related to his desire to make words coincide with concrete physical being. This relationship is illustrated in the following passage from *"Fragmentations."* (The expression "té vé" here means *"bonjour"* in Marseillais slang.)

> And what is the tetema?
>
> It's the blood of the body stretched out at this moment, and which dozes because it [the body] sleeps. How can the tetema be blood? By the *ema,* which is preceded by the resting t which indicates whatever may be resting like the té vé of the people of Marseilles. For the té makes a sound like ashes when the tongue places it between the lips where it will smoke.
>
> And Ema in Greek means blood. And tetema means twice the ashes on the flame of the blood clot. (F, 681)

Artaud begins this passage by implying that word and flesh are one and the same: "tetema" does not stand for blood; it *is* blood. "Ema" and "t" are obviously real entities for Artaud; joined, the resultant combination is stronger than either component by itself. The "té" must also possess a certain strength since it will smoke once it is placed between the lips. The physical strength that Artaud ascribes to these words appears unrelated to their meaning or representational value.

The belief that every word possesses physical strength is at the base of the verbal magic and incantatory rites of primitive peoples. Since Artaud shares this belief it follows that he would attribute magical powers to incantation. Convinced that demonic spirits were casting spells upon him, he fought magic with magic. Through incantations he hoped to exorcize himself of the things he dreaded and despised. In *"Le cahier Lutèce ou le reniement du baptême"* ("The Lutetian Notebook: or, Repudiation of Baptism"), Artaud interrupts a coherent attack on the Catholic Church with a series of incantations. He ends by asserting:

> racavetu o dun dacasjata
> racama racama dombra

it's not enough to say it
but I said it and I say it again
I repudiate baptism
and the preceding incomprehensible words are at the most
curses against the fact of having been baptized.[22]

As he states expressly, Artaud is not using incantations simply for the sound and rhythm of the words. He has recourse
to incantations in the hope that he will thereby rid himself
of Christianity.

Another good example of this deliberate use of incantation is found in the poem *"Ainsi donc la question"* ("Here
then is the question"). After declaring that he alone is responsible for his creation, Artaud cries out that all suffering
will cease and introduces an incantation obviously intended
to exorcize pain and disease:

> therefore no more suffering,
> no more illness
> dysentery
> suffocation . . .
> ka loughin
> re te ka la gouda
> ka lagouda
> e te ka loughin[23]

One incantatory passage contains a number of words which
form an anagram of Artaud's own name, indicating an attempt to exorcize himself of something or someone. Immediately before the incantation, he asserts that opium contains
the secret of an immortal yeast—a secret which has been vio-
lated in the course of orgies held in the Himalayas and
the Caucasus.

> Talachtis talachti tsapoula
> koiman koima nara
> ara trafund arakulda

> which is a rhythm of exorcism against the drying up
> of opium by orgies and consecrations. (R, 34)

This incantation is directed at sexuality (orgies) and spirituality (consecrations)—both of which conspire to rob Artaud of the opium he so desperately needs.

Although it is impossible to analyze most of the words found in Artaud's incantations, certain general remarks can be made. As Eric Sellin notes, many words reflect Artaud's preoccupations: papa, mama, popo pesti *(peste-plague)*, koma (coma), kurbura *(courbature-ache)*, and kana (cane). Still other words are variations on Greek and, more often, Latin words with endings similar to those of Latin declensions—*i, a, um,* and *us,* Finally, it seems highly likely that Artaud drew certain words from historical incantations. He was acquainted with the book *La magie assyrienne: Etude suivi de textes magiques* (published in Paris in 1902), which contains numerous ancient Assyrian incantations that the author–editor, Charles Fossey, had translated into French. Many of the magic syllables found in these incantations crop up in Artaud's poetry. Some of them denote parts of the body and were used in rituals designed to cure sickness and disease: ka (mouth), eme (tongue), ma (womb). Still others refer to the process of exorcism itself: enim-enim-ma (exorcism), ta-mat (be exorcized), tu-tu (incantation). There is no reason to think that Artaud used these syllables with any consistency or deliberation, but it is probable that he remembered some of the more common sounds and incorporated them into his poetry.

Many of Artaud's poems contain long passages composed of violent and obscene words, strung together like a litany of horrors. Although these passages are not incantations in the strict sense of the word, they are used in much the same way. Convinced that language has the capacity to inflict physical hurt, Artaud applies savage and brutal terms to whatever he hates, in the hope of destroying it. This use of violence may also stem from Artaud's belief that literature comes from the body (itself composed of savage drives) and, in addition, must be able to affect the bodies of other men. Unless language is as aggressive as man himself, it cannot accomplish this task. He demands a language which is as brutal as any physical wound. "But if I drive in a violent word like a nail I want it to suppurate in the sentence like a laceration with a hundred holes. You don't reproach a writer for an obscene word because it is obscene, you reproach him for it if it is gratuitous, that is, flat and without magic." (I, 10)

Although many critics have claimed that Artaud's use of violence *is* gratuitous and uncontrolled, the better case is that Artaud employs violent words like incantation, deliberately and calculatedly. In *Ci-gît*, for example, he describes his increasing solitude as faithful friends and allies die. Finally, he comes to the realization that he is surrounded by enemies:

> I had only a few faithful who never stopped dying
> for me.
> When they were too dead to continue living
> they left only those full of hate.

Immediately following this passage, Artaud launches into one far less lucid—a violent attack directed against those whom he hates and fears. Since this diatribe ends as abruptly as it begins, it is obviously deliberate and carefully controlled despite its apparent spontaneity.

> Myrmidons of Infernal Persephone,
> germs of every hollow gesture,

buffoon mucus of a dead law,
cysts of beings who rape each other,
tongues of the greedy
forceps
scratched on its own
                    urine
latrines of bony death

Violence plays a major role in the blasphemous passages frequently found in Artaud's later poems. In *"Main
d'ouvrier et main de singe"* ("Workman's Hand and Monkey's Hand"), he addresses God with words normally considered obscene and pornographic:

    you nasty old tonsured asshole
    and the asshole of your foul backside
    and the opening of your hole-y soul . . .

    the SOUL

    that you wanted to palm off on me
    from the bottom of your hole-y ass . . .

    when your cornholed monkey's hand
    gathered the filth [*le mal*]
    which filled
    your whole ass
    in order to make me
                    throw it
                    all up.[24]

The word *"mal"* obviously has two meanings in this passage:
one is spiritual (evil) and the other scatological (excrement).

Although the incantations and the violent passages in Artaud's poems are probably the most original and personal
element in his work, by no means do they constitute a new
language. Like all of Artaud's puns and word games, they
are meaningful only because, in one way or another, they

are related to discursive language. Artaud could no more create a new language than he could render language real. But he did not submit to the limitations imposed by language without a desperate struggle—a struggle unequaled in the work of any other French writer.

CONCLUSION

Misunderstood during his life, hailed as a prophet after his death, Antonin Artaud shared the fate of the poets he had admired: Poe, Baudelaire, Nerval, and Lautréamont. It did not take long—some twenty years—for an appreciation of the significance of his work to set in. His greatest admirers are not to be found in his native France, where the age-old traditions of rational analysis and Cartesian logic are still much in evidence, but rather in England and, even more so, in the United States. For whom, then, is Artaud a prophet? Certainly for those involved in the theater. But they are not the only ones: Artaud's name is mentioned no less frequently in the underground press than in any literary milieu when questions relevant to language and literature are seriously discussed. These different groups—people of the theater, hippies, writers, and critics—may seem far removed from one another, but, in a sense, they are marked by a similar sensibility. In fact, traditional distinctions between these groups seem to be disappearing: a number of contemporary theatrical companies—the most famous of which is the Living Theater—now resemble "hippie" communities. Both the new theatrical groups and the "underground generation" flee from Western society, supposedly based on rational thought and speech. They seek to liberate man from the stifling conventions and restrictions imposed by society in the hope that he will recover a vital inner peace and harmony. The theater, they argue, does not exist to entertain, but to affect man's very life. More and more, this theater shies away from all that is literary, from written scripts, from words themselves. It views language as the embodiment of the falseness and artificiality, the so-called logic and rationality, which lead to dehumanization, facelessness, and doom. The distrust of Western civilization and the "retreat from the word"—to use a phrase created by George Steiner— pervade not only the theater, but, to a large extent, contemporary literature itself. Samuel Beckett and Henri Michaux are as suspicious of logic and language as Julian Beck and Timothy Leary. It is this shared distrust—of society, of reason, and of language—that attracts these groups to the figure of Antonin Artaud.

First, the theater: This is the domain where Artaud's influence was first felt and is most easily discernible. Numerous important directors, actors, and dramatists acknowledge their debt to Artaud. Jean-Louis Barrault has called *Le théâtre et son double* the most important book written on the theater in the twentieth century. Artaud's name is almost invariably linked with avant-garde theatrical troupes such as Julian and Judith Malina Beck's Living Theater, Jerzy Grotowski's Polish Laboratory Theater, and Peter Brook's Theater of Cruelty in London. Although elements of Artaud's "theater of cruelty" can be seen in the work of today's leading dramatists—Ionesco, Beckett, Genet—only in recent years, according to critic Susan Sontag, has Artaud's concept of theater been fully realized. "We have up to now lacked a full-fledged example of Artaud's category, 'the theater of cruelty.' The closest thing to it are the theatrical events in New York and elsewhere in the last five years, largely by painters (such as Alan Kaprow, Claes Oldenburg, Jim Dine, Bob Whitman, Red Grooms, Robert Watts) and without text or intelligible speech, called Happenings."[1] These Happenings fulfill many of Artaud's major requirements for the theater: they dismiss psychology, emphasize sound and spectacle at the expense of words, and frequently compel audience participation. However, Miss Sontag does fail to mention that Artaud's meta-physical aspirations, so central to *Le théâtre et son double,* are completely lacking in today's Happenings.

Far from lacking recognition, Artaud's influence on the theater may actually be overrated for two reasons. The first of these is that a number of his ideas were hardly new. Nietzsche had demanded that the theater play a metaphysical role years before Artaud spoke of "cosmic cruelty." And in the early part of the century, theoreticians of the theater such as Gordon Craig and Adolphe Appia stressed the important role that sight and sound should play in the theater. But although Artaud did not create new theatrical concepts, he had the undeniable genius to make them come alive in the burning language of poetry. It is impossible to compare an essay such as "The Theater and the Plague" with the theoretical discussions of Appia and Craig. It must not be forgotten that, above all, Artaud was a *poet* who wrote of the theater. The second reason is less arguable: Artaud's ideal theater was essentially unrealizable. Nicola Chiaromonte is the only critic to have seriously analyzed the contradictions inherent in Artaud's concept of drama.

> On the one hand, his theater must strive for spiritual in-tensity and the purity of poetry. On the other, it must cling furiously to the corporeal, to the actual presence, to the brutal and exterior effect. If we separate these drives we re-duce each of them to a series of banal propositions. It seems to me that the source of their significance and evoca-tive power is the spasmodic tension between them and the irresolute immobility resulting from it.[2]

Chiaromonte's observation makes it clear that Artaud's con-cept of the theater mirrors his insoluble inner conflict: Tor-tured by enslavement to his body and a hatred of it, Artaud would first declare that the body was the source of everything, and then express his ardent wish to attain a spiritual state which was free of all corporeality. However, while Artaud's theatrical ideal may have been characterized by his own inner contradictions and for that reason unrealizable, his criticism of existing theater did touch a vital nerve in contemporary civilization. Through his criticism of the contemporary stage, Artaud attacked some of our most fundamental values and beliefs—our reliance on logical thought and our faith in the power of language. Long before the current mistrust and alienation bred by a technological age, Artaud condemned Western society as corrupt and decadent.

In his desire to find a new kind of order, a new kind of faith, Artaud turned, as did other Surrealists, to the "irrational"—to drugs, mysticism, and magic. Other members of the group may have found the occult sciences interesting, but for Artaud nothing could have been more real. In this too, he was the precursor of today's hippies who flee from a life-destroying mass society to seek refuge in an irrational which takes many forms—especially astrology and Eastern mysticism. Discarding the rationalism associated with a dehumanized society, they attempt to find truths which have meaning for the individual. Understandably, Artaud was recognized immediately as a kindred spirit by this alienated segment of our society. The underground press speaks of Artaud in the reverent tones generally reserved for religious leaders. In the Los Angeles Free Press of January 19, 1967, a full-page article devoted to Artaud concludes with the comment that the poet was "a true artist vowed to martyrdom, who dared not to accept the world and searched for inventing [sic] his life, a man whose genius led him to insanity." In San Francisco, the first English edition of Artaud's poetry was published by City Lights Books, and one of his scenarios, *The Philosopher's Stone,* was produced by a theatrical group in Haight-Ashbury.

Rejection of Western society is often accompanied by an unwillingness to place any faith in the power of language. Words are regarded as the instruments of the very same logic and rationality which have been leading us to destruction. But this distrust of language, which has now reached substantial proportions, did not begin with Artaud, or even with the Surrealists. The "crisis of poetic means"—as George Steiner calls it—found its roots in the nineteenth century with Rimbaud and Mallarmé.

It arose from awareness of the gap between the new sense of psychological reality and the old modes of rhetorical and poetic statement. In order to articulate the wealth of consciousness opened to modern sensibility, a number of poets sought to break out of the traditional confines of syntax and definition. Rimbaud, Lautréamont, and Mallarmé strove to restore to language a fluid, provisional character; they hoped to give back to the world the power of incantation— of conjuring up the unprecedented—which it possesses when it is still a form of magic. They realized that traditional syntax organizes our preception into linear and monistic patterns. Such patterns distort or stifle the play of subconscious energies, the multitudinous life of the interior of the mind, as it was revealed by Blake, Dostoevsky, Nietzsche, and Freud.[3]

Steiner emphasizes the fact that the poets he mentions attempted to transcribe new modes of consciousness. It is equally important to remember that they sought also to express spiritual truths. Their quest was essentially a metaphysical one; Rimbaud himself proudly declared, *"J'écrivais des silences, des nuits, je notais l'inexprimable"* (I wrote of silence and night, I observed the inexpressible). How could everyday language—the language of things, of causes and events—express either the ineffable or the complicated inner life of man. In addition, Mallarmé was particularly disturbed by the arbitrary nature of words: Why, he asked, should the word for night *(nuit)* denote night when its sound suggested something quite different. And so he sought to create a poetic language in which sound would correspond to meaning. Furthermore, Mallarmé did not want to evoke things found in the ordinary world, but the essence of each thing, such as it might exist in some kind of Platonic realm. Through poetry, Mallarmé and Rimbaud sought, albeit in different ways, to transcend ordinary reality and make contact with Being itself. Their quest was doomed to failure and, as Nathan Scott observes, they fell into a "profound despair of language and literature, for what had been sought was an ultimacy of Being that had necessarily to be betrayed by the concretions of verbal discourse."[4] Unable to raise poetry to the lofty heights they had reserved for it, they began to question the value of literature. Rimbaud abandoned poetry at the age of nineteen, while Mallarmé's poems became increasingly more tortuous and incomprehensible. Nearly a century later, their failure was relived by Artaud, who was to declare that *"toute l'écriture est de la cochonnerie"* (all writing is filthy).

The inadequacy of language which had so tortured Rimbaud and Mallarmé has become more acute than ever in our century. Claiming Rimbaud as a spiritual forerunner, the Surrealists hungered after a "surreality"; at the same time, they wanted to probe the hidden depths of the human psyche, whose existence had but lately been revealed by Freud. "Automatic writing" was to express the deepest substratum of man's being. Convinced that rational thought and normal discourse masked essential truths, the Surrealists fled from logic. They made abundant use of words and images which, although seemingly meaningless, possessed the power to elicit particular responses from the reader—responses that often lie buried deep beneath surface rationality. The Surrealists' experiments with language were matched, if not surpassed, by those of James Joyce. Unable to make literature coincide with life, Joyce created a masterpiece in which language, by creating its own universe, became a substitute for reality. "Indeed, in *Finnegans Wake* the line that divides the novel as a work of art from the living realities of experience is stretched so thinly that Joyce's medium virtually ceases altogether to be that of the English language, as he attempts to make his book become a surrogate for the undifferentiated flux of the phenomenal world."[5]

No less than literary men, philosophers have been absorbed by the crisis of language. Heidegger wanted to rediscover original language and the authentic words which were in touch with actual being. He held that modern language, severed from the roots of being, has been reduced to the level of "chatter," of meaningless utterances. At the opposite end of the philosophical spectrum is the British school of philosophy which has also been interested in problems of language, although its approach is quite different. Wittgenstein, in many ways the founder of both logical positivism and linguistic analysis, raised fundamental questions concerning the nature of meaning, the way reality is represented in words, the relationship between the language we use and our inner sensations and mental states, and the multiple roles that words can play. Of Wittgenstein and Heidegger, Erich Heller observes:

And there is a historical sense in which the two extremes of contemporary philosophizing—Heidegger's tortuous metaphysical probings into language and Wittgenstein's absorption in language-games . . . can be seen as two aspects of the same intention: to track down to their source in language and there to correct the absurdities of human endeavor to speak the truth.[6]

Lastly, a contemporary French novelist–philosopher, Maurice Blanchot, approaches the problem of language from a literary viewpoint. For Blanchot, the nature of literature is such that it tends toward disappearance and, ultimately, silence.

The term "silence" is an important one, for Blanchot is by no means the only observer to have applied it to contemporary writing. In his book titled *The New Literature,* Claude Mauriac comments, "After the silence of Rimbaud, the blank page of Mallarmé, the inarticulate cry of Artaud, a literature finally dissolves in alliteration with Joyce."[7] And in his analysis of Samuel Beckett, Mauriac suggests that this Irish writer has reached a point where writing itself is no longer conceivable. Samuel Beckett, and Henry Miller along with him, are the two principal authors examined by Ihab Hassan in his book whose very title is *The Literature of Silence.*[8] Hassan also traces our current crisis of literature back to Mallarmé and Rimbaud who, he says, represented two completely opposed attitudes toward the art of writing. Whereas Mallarmé retreated more and more into estheticism and hermeticism, making his language move toward silence and disappearance, Rimbaud insisted that literature be a means of action. But whether one chooses estheticism or action, whether one sides with Mallarmé and Samuel Beckett or with Rimbaud and Henry Miller, the end is the same: the rejection of literature as we know it. If literature becomes either silence or action, it is perforce obliged to transform itself into something other than literature. In this sense, Mallarmé and Rimbaud heralded the current disillusion with the value of literary creation.

Hassan's major concern is the reaction of the writer when, like the theatrical men or the hippies discussed earlier, he is confronted with the emptiness of contemporary Western civilization and the irrelevancy of literary creation. The writer's desperation may lead to metaphysical revolt—a revolt which often takes the form of violence and obscenity in his work. Or, he may show his contempt for literature by turning it into a game—into a series of permutations in the manner of Beckett.

More than any other modern writer—with the possible exception of Henri Michaux—Artaud has embraced these various attitudes. This is not to say that he accepted them as a parlor intellectual; he lived them in the flesh and marrow of his body. And it is for this reason that Artaud is of great interest to those who care about the future of language and literature. Constantly questioning the value and meaning of writing, Artaud rejected the idea that literature could be created for entertainment or for any purpose other than to express man's ultimate concerns. If he wanted words to come from the body it was because he hoped that, in this way, literature would finally coincide with life itself. Along with other Surrealists, he at first thought that automatic writing and poetic images could reveal the hidden depths of consciousness. He was shortly to declare, however, that language and words could never coincide with being and life. Words would always be used arbitrarily, they would always screen what they had been chosen to reveal. So Artaud turned to painting, to film, to the theater—all in the hope that plastic images, gestures, lights, and sounds would prove less traitorous, less arbitrary, than words. For some time he thought that the "physical" language of the stage or of the Mexican terrain could coincide with being. The natural configurations of the Mexican landscape spoke to him of metaphysics, of man, of life itself. And he felt that his own body corresponded to nature, that his body was like the "mountain of signs." Nature had spoken and an intimate harmony existed between the language of the body and that of the mountains and rocks. Here man had rediscovered his role in the cosmos.

But Artaud could no more stay in Mexico than he could live on stage, and upon his return to Europe he was faced again with the verbal language he so despised.

At no time was Artaud prepared to accept language and poetry on their own terms. Instead, he tried to turn literature into something that was not literature. The violence and obscenity which characterize the poems he wrote before his death bespeak more than a metaphysical revolt against the limitations imposed by the human condition. They reveal Artaud's revolt against literature itself. He wanted his poems to become part of the violence of the body, like a physical wound, like the cry of a man in agony. In a desperate attempt to make language real, to render it as tangible and efficacious as a physical object, Artaud had recourse to incantation. Nevertheless, the more he tried to turn language into a means of action, the more Artaud was compelled to realize the futility of his efforts. However disappointed he may have been at times, Artaud never really lost all hope of writing poetry that would affect the bodies and lives of other men. His last poem, *Pour en finir avec le jugement de dieu,* was to transform man's nervous system so that he could attain a "new, unusual and radiant Epiphany in the sky." Whatever Artaud's intention, the originality and power of his last poems do not come from the creation of a language capable of action, but from the intensity of his own vision—from the anguish, despair, and terror that was Antonin Artaud.

NOTES

CHAPTER I

1. Most of the biographical data concerning Artaud has been drawn from Paule Thévenin's article, "Artaud: 1896–1948," in *Cahiers de la Compagnie Madeleine Renaud—Jean-Louis Barrault*, No. 22–23 (May, 1958), 17–46.

2. See Pierre Chaleix, *"Avant le surréalisme: Artaud chez le Dr. Toulouse,"* *La Tour de Feu*, No. 63–64 (December, 1959), 55–60.

3. Charles Dullin, *"Lettre à Roger Blin,"* *K, Revue de la Poésie*, No. 1–2 (June, 1948), 22.

4. Jean-Louis Barrault, *"L'homme théâtre . . . ,"* *Cahiers de la Compagnie Madeleine Renaud—Jean-Louis Barrault*, No. 22–23 (May, 1958), 48.

5. Jean Hort, *Antonin Artaud, le suicidé de la société* (Geneva: Editions, Connaître, 1960), pp. 56, 58, 67.

6. *"Conversation avec André Masson,"* *Cahiers de la Compagnie Madelaine Renaud—Jean-Louis Barrault*, No. 22–23 (May, 1958), 11, 13.

7. André Breton, *Entretiens: 1913–1952* (Paris: Gallimard, 1952), p. 109.

8. *Ibid.*, p. 110.

9. *Ibid.*, p. 108.

10. *"Au grand jour,"* in Maurice Nadeau's *Histoire du surréalisme*, II (Paris: Seuil, 1948), pp. 96–97.

11. André Breton, *Les manifestes du surréalisme*, Collection *Idées* (Paris: Gallimard, 1963), pp. 84–85.

12. *Diary of Anaïs Nin, 1931–1934* (New York: Swallow Press & Harcourt, Brace & World, 1966), p. 187.

13. Anaïs Nin, *Under a Glass Bell* (New York: Dutton, 1948), p. 48.

14. See Thévenin, "Artaud," 29.

15. Quoted in Thévenin, 29–30.

16. *"Lettre à Anaïs Nin,"* *Tel Quel*, No. 20 (Winter, 1965), 8.

17. *Diary of Anaïs Nin*, p. 229.

18. *Ibid.*

19. Breton, *Manifestes*, p. 24.

20. *Diary of Anaïs Nin*, pp. 192–193.

21. *Ibid.*

22. Pierre Jean Jouve, *"Les Cenci,"* *la Nouvelle Revue Française*, No. 261 (June, 1935), 912.

23. Manuel Cano de Castro, *"Rencontre d'Artaud avec les Tarots,"* *K, Revue de la Poésie*, No. 1–2 (June, 1948), 119–121.

24. *Lettres d'Antonin Artaud à*

Jean-Louis Barrault (Paris: Bordas, 1952), p. 117.

25. Quoted in Charles Marowitz, "Artaud at Rodez," *Evergreen Review*, April, 1968, 66.

26. Quoted in Thévenin, "Artaud," 39.

27. Quoted in Gaston Ferdière, "J'ai soigné Antonin Artaud," *La Tour de Feu*, No. 63–64 (December, 1959), 31.

28. "Electro-choc," *Les Temps Modernes*, No. 40 (February, 1949), 217.

29. Ferdière, "J'ai soigné Antonin Artaud," 28–38.

30. Quoted in Jacques Latrémolière, "J'ai parlé de Dieu avec Antonin Artaud," *La Tour de Feu*, No. 69 (April, 1961), 23.

31. Quoted in Latrémolière, 22.

32. François Mauriac, "Bloc-Notes," *l'Express*, December 3, 1959, 44.

33. Marie-Ange Malausséna, "Notes bio-biographiques," *La Tour de Feu*, No. 63–64 (December, 1959), 82.

34. "André Breton parle d'Artaud pour La Tour de Feu," *La Tour de Feu*, No. 63–64 (December, 1959), 4.

35. Maurice Saillet, "Tête-à-tête avec Antonin Artaud," *K, Revue de la Poésie*, No. 1–2 (June, 1948), 105.

36. "Lettre à Maurice Saillet," *K, Revue de la Poésie*, 108.

37. André Gide, "Témoignage," *84*, No. 5–6 (1948), 151.

38. *Tulane Drama Review*, IX, No. 3 (Spring, 1965), 99–117.

CHAPTER II

1. Gaëtan Picon, *L'usage de la lecture*, Vol. II (Paris: Mercure de France, 1961), p. 191.

2. Maurice Blanchot, *Le livre à venir* (Paris: Gallimard, 1959), p. 51.

3. Stephen Koch, "On Artaud," *Tri-Quarterly*, No. 6 (Spring, 1966), 33.

4. *Ibid.*, 34.

5. Nin, *Under a Glass Bell*, p. 50.

6. *Ibid.*, p. 55.

7. Otto Hahn, *Portrait d'Antonin Artaud* (Paris: Le Soleil Noir, 1968), p. 38.

8. *Ibid.*, p. 53.

9. Breton, *Manifestes*, p. 184.

10. *Ibid.*, p. 92.

11. Maurice Blanchot, *La part du feu* (Paris: Gallimard, 1949), p. 103.

12. Breton, *Manifestes*, p. 37.

13. Breton, *Point du jour* (Paris: Gallimard, 1934), p. 24.

14. Breton, *Manifestes*, p. 46.

15. *Ibid.*, p. 109.

16. Nicola Chiaromonte, "Antonin Artaud," *Encounter*, XXXIX (August, 1967), 44–45.

17. Breton, *Manifestes*, p. 51.

18. *Ibid.*

19. Alain Virmaux analyzes Artaud's relationship to important directors of this era such as Buñuel and Cocteau. See the *Tulane Drama Review*, XI, No. 1 (Fall, 1966), 154–165.

20. Maurice Blanchot, "Le demain joueur," and Octavio Paz,

"André Breton ou la recherche du commencement," la Nouvelle Revue Française, No. 172 (April, 1967), 863–888; 606–619.

21. Michel Carrouges, "Surréalisme et occultisme," Cahiers d'Hermès, No. 2 (Paris: Editions du Vieux Colombier, 1947), 194–218. See also his book, André Breton et les données fondamentales du surréalisme, Collection Idées (Paris: Gallimard, 1967).

22. See Ferdinand Alquié, Philosophie du surréalisme (Paris: Flammarion, 1956), esp. pp. 37, 159.

23. Breton, Manifestes, pp. 76–77.

24. Breton, Entretiens, p. 283.

25. Swami Prabhavananda and Frederick Manchester, The Spiritual Heritage of India, Anchor Book (New York: Doubleday, 1964), p. xiii.

26. Eduard Zeller, Outlines of the History of Greek Philosophy (New York: Meridian, 1955), p. 32.

27. Artaud, "L'éperon malicieux, le double-cheval," Botteghe Oscure, No. 8 (1951), 11.

CHAPTER III

1. Alquié, Philosophie du surréalisme, p. 78.

2. "The Artaud Experiment," Tulane Drama Review, VIII, No. 2 (Winter, 1963), 21.

3. Alan Seymour, "Artaud's Cruelty," London Magazine, III, No. 12 (March, 1964), 59–64.

4. Chiaromonte, "Artaud," 46.

5. Nin, Under a Glass Bell, pp. 50–51.

6. Breton, Entretiens, p. 235.

7. Ibid., p. 279.

8. Ibid., p. 248.

9. Octavio Paz, "André Breton ou la recherche du commencement," 609.

10. Claude Lévi-Strauss, Structural Anthropology, trans. by Claire Jacobson and Brooke Grundfest Schoepf, Anchor Book (New York: Doubleday, 1967), p. 206.

11. A leading contemporary philosopher seems to agree with Artaud's distinction between "culture" and "civilization." See Susanne Langer, Philosophical Sketches, Mentor Book (New York: New American Library, 1964), Chapter VI.

12. Ernst Cassirer, The Philosophy of Symbolic Forms, Vol. II: Mythical Thought (New Haven: Yale University Press, 1955), p. 38.

13. Ibid., p. 55.

14. Ibid., p. 81.

15. Ibid., pp. 188–189.

16. Lévi-Strauss, Structural Anthropology, p. 227.

17. Kurt Seligman, The History of Magic (New York: Pantheon, 1948), p. 129.

18. Chiaromonte, "Artaud," 46.

19. Swami Nikhilananda, ed., The Upanishads, Torchbook (New York: Harper & Row, 1963), p. 33.

20. See Gershom Scholem, Major Trends in Jewish Mysticism (3rd ed.; New York: Schocken, 1961).

21. Martin Heidegger, *An Introduction to Metaphysics*, Anchor Book (New York: Doubleday, 1961), p. 11.

22. *Ibid.*, p. 144.

23. Heidegger, "Hölderlin and the Essence of Poetry," in *Existence and Being*, Gateway Edition (Chicago: Henry Regnery Co., 1949), p. 283.

24. Jerzy Grotowski, *"Il n'était pas entièrement lui-même,"* *Les Temps Modernes*, No. 251 (April, 1967), 1890.

25. Chiaromonte, "Artaud," 50.

26. Hahn, *Portrait d'Artaud*, p. 66.

27. Chiaromonte, "Artaud," 49.

28. Friedrich Nietzsche, *The Birth of Tragedy*, Anchor Book (New York: Doubleday, 1956), p. 94.

CHAPTER IV

1. Koch, "On Artaud," 36.

2. *Ibid.*

3. *"L'homme et sa douleur,"* *La Tour de Feu*, No. 69 (April, 1961), 9.

4. *"Lettre à Peter Watson,"* *Critique*, October, 1948, 873.

5. *"Les sentiments retardent . . . ,"* *Les Lettres Nouvelles*, No. 42 (October, 1956), 370.

6. *Ibid.*

7. Koch, "On Artaud," 37.

8. *"Fragments,"* *l'Arche*, No. 16 (1946), 42.

9. *"Notes sur la peinture,"* *Tel Quel*, No. 15 (Autumn, 1963), 75.

10. *"Textes,"* *Le Disque Vert*, No. 4 (1953), 41.

11. *"Le visage humain,"* in *Portraits et dessins* (Paris: Galerie Pierre, 1947), no pagination.

12. *"Lettre à Watson,"* 869.

13. *Autre chose que de l'enfant beau* (Paris: Broder, 1957), no pagination.

14. *Révolte contre la poésie* (Paris: Friends of the Author, 1944), no pagination.

15. Jacques Derrida, *"La parole soufflée,"* *Tel Quel*, No. 20 (Winter, 1965), 57.

16. *"Le théâtre et la science,"* *Théâtre populaire*, No. 5 (January-February, 1954), 5.

17. *"Sur les* Chimères," *Tel Quel*, No. 22 (Summer, 1963), 5.

18. *"Extraits des 'Suppôts et supplications [sic],' "* *La Nef*, No. 71–72 (December, 1950-January, 1951), 22.

19. Eric Sellin, *The Dramatic Concepts of Antonin Artaud* (University of Chicago Press, 1968), p. 89.

20. Seligman, *History of Magic*, p. 353.

21. *Ibid.*, p. 358.

22. *"Le cahier Lutèce ou le reniement du baptême,"* *La Tour de Feu*, No. 69 (April, 1961), 36–37.

23. *"Ainsi donc la question,"* *Tel Quel*, No. 30 (Summer, 1967), 17.

24. *K, Revue de la Poésie*, No. 1–2 (June, 1948), 5.

CONCLUSION

1. Susan Sontag, *Against Interpretation*, Delta Book (New York: Dell, 1967), p. 172.

2. Chiaromonte, "Artaud," 50.

3. George Steiner, *Language and Silence* (New York: Atheneum, 1967), p. 27.

4. Nathan Scott, *Samuel Beckett* (London: Bowes & Bowes, 1965), p. 17.

5. *Ibid.*, p. 69.

6. Erich Heller, "Ludwig Wittgenstein," *Encounter,* No. 72 (September, 1959), 45.

7. Claude Mauriac, *The New Literature,* trans. by Samuel I. Stone (New York: Braziller, 1959), p. 12.

8. Ihab Hassan, *The Literature of Silence,* Borzoi Book (New York: Knopf, 1967).

BIBLIOGRAPHY

Chronological List of Artaud's Works

Oeuvres complètes. 7 volumes. Paris: Gallimard, 1956–1967. *Supplément au Tome I,* 1970.

"*Boutique de l'âme.*" *CAP,* No. 1 1924).

"*Lettre à personne.*" *Cashiers du Sud,* No. 31 (July, 1926) 5–6.

Ludwig Lewisohn. *Crime passionnel.* Translated by Artaud in collaboration with Bernard Steele. Paris: Denoël & Steele, 1932.

"*Le livre de Monelle.*" *Gazette des Amis des Livres,* April, 1939.

Révolte contre la poésie. Paris: Friends of the Author, 1944.

"*Le bébé de feu.*" Translation of an English poem by Robert Southwell. *Poésie 44,* No. 20 (1944), 21–22.

D'un voyage au pays des Tarahumaras. Collection "L'Age d'Or." Paris: Fontaine, 1945. Reprinted in 1963 by Arbalète (Isère) under the title of *Les Tarahumaras.*

"*Fragments.*" *l'Heure nouvelle,* No. 1 (1945), 51–52.

Lettres de Rodez. Paris: GLM, 1946. Second printing in 1948.

Xylophonie contre la grande presse et son petit public. In collaboration with Henri Pichette. Containing Artaud's "*Histoire entre la groume et Dieu.*" Paris: Impr. Davy, 1946.

"*Les mères à l'étable.*" *l'Heure nouvelle,* No. 2 (1946), 53–55.

"*Lettre sur Lautréamont.*" *Cahiers du Sud,* No. 275 (1946), 6–10.

"*Centre-noeuds.*" *Juin,* No. 18 (June, 1946), 4.

"*Lettre à Adamov.*" *l'Arch,* No. 16 (June, 1946), 38–39.

"*Le théâtre et l'anatomie.*" *La Rue,* July, 1946.

"*Lettre à Colette Thomas.*" *Les Lettres,* No. 22 (October, 1946), 50–54.

"*Centre pitere et potron chier.*" *Troisième Convoi,* No. 3 (November, 1946), 21–33.

Artaud le Momo. Paris: Bordas, 1947.

Portraits et dessins. Containing the poem "*Le visage humain.*" Paris: Galerie Pierre, 1947.

Ci-gît, précédé de la culture indienne. Paris: K, 1947.

Van Gogh, le suicidé de la société. Paris: K, 1947.

"Les malades et les médecins." Quatre Vents, No. 8 (1947), 15–20.

"La magre à la condition la même et magre à l'inconditionné." 84, No. 1 (1947), 1–3.

"Van Gogh." 84, No. 2 (1947).

"L'intempestive mort et L'aveu *d'Arthur Adamov." Cahiers de la Pléiade*, April, 1947, 138–140.

"L'arve et l'aune." Arbalète, No. 12 (Spring, 1947), 161–184.

Pour en finir avec le jugement de dieu. Paris: K, 1948.

"Lettre à Peter Watson." Critique, October, 1948, 867–874

"Aliéner l'acteur"; "Le théâtre et la science." Arbalète, No. 13 (Summer, 1948), 7–14; 15–24.

"Paris-Varsovie." 84, No. 3–4 (1948), 55–57.

"Poèmes inédits." 84, No. 5–6 (1948), 97–136.

"Le chevalier Mate-Tapis." Adaptation of a poem by Lewis Carroll. *Cahiers du Sud*, No. 287 (1948), 2.

"Main d'ouvrier et main de singe"; "Lettres"; "Il fallait d'abord avoir envie de vivre." K. Revue de la Poésie, No. 1–2 (June, 1948).

"Lettre d'Antonin Artaud à Marcel Bataille"; "Fragment d'un poème inédit." France-Asie, No. 30 (September, 1948), 1051–1058.

Supplément aux Lettres de Rodez suivi de Coleridge le traître. Paris: GLM, 1949.

Lettre contre la Cabbale. Paris: Jacques Haumont, 1949.

"Il y a une vieille histoire." 84, No. 7 (1949), 156–157.

"Notes"; "Je hais et abjecte en lâche." 84, No. 8–9 (1949), 278–284.

"C'est qu'un jour"; "L'erreur est dans le fait." 84, No. 10–11 (1949), 404–408.

"Moi Antonin Artaud." Poésie des mots inconnus. 1949.

"Extraits des 'Suppôts et suppliciations.'" Les Temps Modernes, No. 40 (February, 1949), 217–229.

"Là où j'en suis." Cahiers de la Pléiade, Spring, 1949, 131–139.

"La mort et l'homme." 84, No. 13 (1950), 8.

"Je vois le drame du mâle et de la femelle." In Jacques Prével's *Le livre de colère et de haine.* Paris: Editions du Lion, 1950.

"Lettre." Paragone, No. 8 (August, 1950), 50.

"Je n'ai jamais rien étudié." 84, No. 16 (December, 1950), 11–20.

"Extraits des 'Suppôts et suppliciations.'" La Nef, No. 71–72 (December, 1950–January, 1951), 20–23.

"Trois lettres addresées à des médecins"; "L'éperon malicieux." Botteghe Oscure*, No. 8 (1951), 11–33.

"Sur le Yoga." 84, No. 18 (May-June, 1951), 17–19.

Lettres d'Antonin Artaud à Jean-Louis Barrault. Paris: Bordas, 1952.

"Commentaire sur un conte de Marcel Béalu." In Marcel Béalu's *La bouche ouverte.* Paris: Impr. Blanchet, 1952.

"Lettre." la Revue théâtrale, No. 20 (1952), 7–11.

"Lettre à André Breton." Le Soleil, Noir, Positions, No. 1 (February, 1952), 53–56.

"L'amour à Changaï." Voir, No. 429 (December, 1952), 4.

"Lettre." La Revue Théâtrale, No. 20 (1952), 7–11.

La vie et mort de Satan le feu. Paris: Arcanes, 1953.

"Textes inédits." Le Disque Vert, No. 4 (1953), 37–49.

"Deux textes sur la musique." Cahiers de la Compagnie Madeleine Renaud—Jean-Louis Barrault, No. 3 (1954), 66–68.

Galapagos. Paris: Broder, 1955.

"Trois lettres inédites." la Revue théâtrale, No. 32 (1956), 7–13.

"Notes complémentaires aux Nouvelles révélations de l'être. Entretiens, No. 6 (Summer, 1956), 1–14.

"Les sentiments retardent." Les Lettres Nouvelles, No. 42 (October, 1956), 369–373.

Autre chose que de l'enfant beau. Paris: Broder, 1957.

Voici un endroit. Paris: PAB, 1958.

"Lettre à Pierre Loeb." Les Lettres Nouvelles, No. 59 (April, 1958), 481–486.

"Lettre à Henri Thomas." Cahier des Saisons, No. 16 (Spring, 1959), 97–99.

"Trois lettres à Ferdière." La Tour de Feu, No. 63–64 (December, 1959), 6–16.

"Lettre à Camus." la Nouvelle Revue Française, No. 89 (May, 1960), 1012–1020.

"Chiote à l'esprit." Tel Quel, No. 3 (Fall, 1960), 3–9.

"Lettre à Paulhan." la Nouvelle Revue Française, No. 95 (November, 1960), 982–988.

"Fragmentations." Les Temps Modernes, January, 1961, 678–688.

"Lettre à Roger Karl." Lettre ouverte, No. 2 (March, 1961), 59–61.

"L'homme et sa douleur"; "Lettres à Latrémolière"; "Cahier Lutèce." La Tour de Feu, No. 69 (April, 1961), 9–38.

México. Mexico: Universidad Nacional Autónoma de México, 1962.

"Dédicace à Jacques Prével." la Nouvelle Revue Française, May, 1962, 582–584.

"Une note sur la peinture surréaliste." Tel Quel, No. 15 (Fall, 1963), 75–79.

"Lettre à Alfredo Gangotena." la Nouvelle Revue Française, No. 149 (May, 1965), 941–943.

"Sur les Chimères." *Tel Quel,* No. 22 (Summer, 1965). 3–14.

"Notes de mise en scène d'Antonin Artaud pour Les Cenci." Cahiers de la Compagnie Madeleine Renaud—Jean-Louis Barrault, No. 51 (November, 1965), 20–38.

"Onze lettres à Anaïs Nin." Tel Quel. No. 20 (Winter, 1965), 3–12.

"Ainsi donc la question." Tel Quel, No. 30 (Summer, 1967), 12–22.

"Il y a dans la magie." Tel Quel, No. 35 (Autumn, 1968), 90–95.

Lettres à Génica Athanasiou. Collection "Le point du jour." Paris: Gallimard, 1969.

"La main de singe"; "l'amour est un arbre qui est toujours monté"; "Chanson." Tel Quel, No. 39 (Autumn, 1969), 13–30.

Works by Artaud Translated into English

"Van Gogh: The Man Suicided by Society." Translated by Bernard Frechtman. *The Tiger's Eye,* No. 7 (March, 1949), 93–115. Reprinted in *The Trembling Lamb* (New York: John Fles, n.d.)

"It isn't possible that in the end the miracle may not occur . . ." *Origin: A Quarterly for the Creative,* No. 11 (Fall, 1953), 131

"Seven Short Poems." Translated by Kenneth Rexroth. *The Black Mountain Review,* I, No. 2 (Summer, 1954), 8–11.

The Theater and Its Double. Translated by Mary C. Richards. New York: Grove Press, 1958.

"Letters from Rodez." Translated by E. S. Seldon. *Evergreen Review,* IV, No. 11 (January-February, 1960), 60–84.

"Three Letters by Antonin Artaud." Translated by T. Fitzsimmons. *Evergreen Review,* VII, No. 28 (January-February, 1963), 52–61.

"States of Mind: 1921–1945." Letters and texts translated by Ruby Cohn. *Tulane Drama Review,* VIII, No. 2 (Winter, 1963), 30–74.

"The Tree." Translated by Paul Zweig. *Chelsea,* No. 13 (June, 1963), 20.

"To Have Done with the Judgment of God." Translated by G. Wernham. *Northwest Review,* VI, No. 4 (Fall, 1963), 45–72.

"Letter to Louis Jouvet"; "To End God's Judgment"; "The Philosopher's Stone"; "Symbolic Mountains." Translated by Victor Corti. *Tulane Drama Review,* IX, No. 3 (Spring, 1965), 56–98.

Artaud Anthology. Edited by Jack Hirshman. San Francisco: City Lights Books, 1965.

"Scenarios and Arguments." *Translated by Victor Corti and Simone* Sanzenbach. *Tulane Drama Review,* XI, No. 1 (Fall, 1966), 166–185.

Black Poet and Other Texts. Introduction and translation by Paul Zweig. Collection "Passeport." Paris: Minard, 1966.

Collected Works. Vol. I. Introduction and translation by Victor Corti. London: Calder & Boyars, 1968.

Selected Secondary Sources

Adamov, Arthur, "*Introduction à Antonin Artaud.*" *Paru,* No. 29 (April, 1947), 7–13.

Alquié, Ferdinand, *Philosophie du surréalisme.* Paris: Flammarion, 1955.

Armand-Laroche, Dr. J. L., *Antonin Artaud et son double.* Périgeux: Fanlac, 1964.

Arnold, Paul, "*Antonin Artaud et le théâtre de la nouvelle vague.*" *Revue Générale Belge,* January, 1960, 75–85.

"Artaud for Artaud's sake." *Encore,* May-June, 1964, 20–32.

Balakian, Anna, *Surrealism: The Road to the Absolute.* New York: Noonday Press, 1959.

Barrault, Jean-Louis, *Réflexions sur le théâtre.* Paris: Vautrain, 1949.

Blanchot, Maurice, *Le livre à venir.* Paris: Gallimard, 1959.

———— *La part du feu.* Paris: Gallimard, 1949.

———— "Artaud." *la Nouvelle Revue Française,* No. 47 (November, 1956), 873–881.

Bonneton, Dr. André, *Le naufrage prophétique d'Antonin Artaud.* Paris: Lefebvre, 1961.

Boschère, Jean de, "*Une âme trop vaste.*" *Cahiers du Sud,* XXXVI, No. 316 (1952), 420–426.

Bosquet, Alain, "*Antonin Artaud ou la vocation de délire.*" *Revue de Paris,* March, 1959, 95–105.

Breton, André, *La clé des champs.* Paris: Sagittaire, 1953.

———— *Entretiens: 1913–1952.* Paris: Gallimard, 1952.

————*Les manifestes du surréalisme.* Collection Idées. Paris: Gallimard, 1963.

———— *Point du jour.* Paris: Gallimard, 1934.

Brustein, Robert, *The Theater of Revolt.* Boston: Little, Brown & Co., 1964.

Burucoa, Christiane, "*Antonin Artaud ou la Difficulté d'être.*" *Entretiens sur les lettres et les arts,* No. 9 (Spring, 1957), 19–25.

Cahiers de la Compagnie Madeleine Renaud—Jean-Louis Barrault: No.

22–23 (May, 1958). Issue entitled *"Antonin Artaud et le théâtre de notre temps."*

Carrouges, Michel, *André Breton et les données fondamentales du surréalisme.* Collection Idées. Paris: Gallimard, 1967.

———— *"Surréalisme et occultisme."* *Cahiers d'Hermès,* No. 2 (1947), 194–218.

Cassirer, Ernst, *The Philosophy of Symbolic Forms.* Vol. I: *Language.* Vol. II: *Mythical Thought.* New Haven: Yale University Press, 1966.

Caws, Mary Ann, "Artaud's Myth of Motion." *French Review,* XLI, No. 4 (February, 1968), 532–538.

Chiaromonte, Nicola, "Antonin Artaud." *Encounter,* XXXIX, No. 2 (August, 1967), 44–50.

Cleyet, George, "Artaud: cry, shout and feel with all of us." Los Angeles *Free Press,* January 19, 1967, 18.

Cohn, Ruby, "Surrealism and Today's French Theater." *Yale French Studies,* No. 31 (May, 1964), 159–166.

Collomp, Alain, *"Antonin Artaud: De la maladie à l'oeuvre."* Unpublished dissertation, University of Paris, 1963.

Cumont, Franz, *Oriental Religions in Roman Paganism.* New York: Dover, 1956.

Decaunes, Luc, *"Les miroirs de l'écriture—à propos d'un nouveau messie."* *Cahiers du Sud,* XXVIII, No. 291 (1948), 365–370.

Derrida, Jacques, *"La parole souflée."* *Tel Quel,* No. 20 (Winter, 1965), 41–68.

———— *"Le théâtre de la cruauté et la clôture de la représentation."* *Critique,* No. 230 (July, 1966), 595–618.

Desternes, Jean, *"Ci-gît Antonin Artaud."* *La Table Ronde,* April, 1948, 692–698.

84, No. 5–6 (1948). Issue entitled "Antonin Artaud."

Esslin, Martin, "The Theater of Cruelty." *New York Times Magazine,* March 4, 1966, pp. 22–23, 71–74.

———— "Violence in Drama." *Encore,* No. 49 (May-June, 1964), 6-16.

Ferdière, Gaston, *"La femme à Roudoudou—Un photomontage d'Antonin Artaud."* *Figaro Littéraire,* September 2, 1961, 4.

Fossey, Charles, *La magie assyrienne.* Paris: Leroux, 1902.

Fowlie, Wallace, *Dionysus in Paris.* New York Meridian, 1960.

———— "The New French Theater: Artaud, Beckett, Genet, Ionesco." *Sewanee Review,* LXVII, No. 4 (Autumn, 1959), 643–657.

France-Asie, No. 30 (1948). Issue entitled *"Hommage à Antonin Artaud."*

Frank, André, "Antonin Artaud." *la Revue théâtrale,* No. 13 (Summer, 1950), 26-37.

Goodman, Paul, "Obsessed by Theater." *The Nation.* November 29, 1958, 412-414.

Grotowski, Jerzy, *"Il n'était pas entièrement lui-même." Les Temps Modernes,* No. 251 (April, 1967), 1885—1893.

Hahn, Otto, *Portrait d'Antonin Artaud.* Paris: Le Soleil Noir, 1968.

Hassan, Ihab, *The Literature of Silence.* Borzoi Book. New York: Knopf, 1967.

Heidegger, Martin, *Existence and Being.* Gateway Edition. Chicago: Henry Regnery Co., 1949.

——— *An Introduction to Metaphysics.* Anchor Book. New York: Doubleday, 1961.

Heller, Erich, "Ludwig Wittgenstein." *Encounter,* No. 72 (September 1959), 40-48.

Hivnor, Mary Otis, "Barrault and Artaud." *Partisan Review,* March, 1948, 332-339.

Hort, Jean, *Antonin Artaud, le suicidé de la société.* Geneva: Editions Connâitre, 1960.

Jouhandeau, Marcel, *Carnets de l'écrivain.* Paris: Gallimard, 1957.

Jouve, Pierre Jean, *"Les Cenci." la Nouvelle Revue Française,* No. 261 (June, 1935), 910-915.

K, Revue de la Poésie, No. 1-2 (June, 1948). Issue entitled "Antonin Artaud."

Kitchin, Laurence, "The Theater of Cruelty." *The Listener,* LXX, No. 1799 (September 19, 1963), 87-89.

Knapp, Bettina, *Antonin Artaud: Man of Vision.* New York: David Lewis, 1969.

——— "Artaud: A New Type of Magic." *Yale French Studies,* No. 31 (May, 1964), 88-99.

Koch, Stephen, "On Artaud." *Tri-Quarterly,* No. 6 (Spring, 1966), 29-37.

Kustow, Michael. *"Sur les traces d'Artaud." Esprit,* No. 338 (May, 1965), 958-964.

Kyrou, Ado, *Le surréalisme au cinéma.* Paris: Arcanes, 1953.

Langer, Susanne, *Philosophical Sketches.* Mentor Book. New York: New American Library, 1964.

——— *Philosophy in a New Key.* Mentor Book. New York: New American Library, 1942.

Laporte, Roger, *"Antonin Artaud ou la pensée au supplice." Le Nouveau Commerce,* No. 12 (Winter, 1968), 21-36.

Lévi-Strauss, Claude, *Structural Anthropology*. Translated by Claire Jacobson and Brooke Grundfest Schoepf. Anchor Book. New York: Doubleday, 1967.

Magny, Olivier de, *"Ecriture de l'impossible."* *Les Lettres Nouvelles*, No. 32 (February, 1963), 125–139.

Malausséna, Marie-Ange, "Antonin Artaud." *la Revue théâtrale*, No. 23 (1953), 39–57.

Marowitz, Charles, "Artaud at Rodez." *Evergreen Review*, April, 1968, pp. 65–67, 81–85.

Matthews, J. H., "Surrealism and the Cinema." *Criticism*, IV, No. 2 (Spring, 1962), 123–134.

Mauriac, Claude, *The New Literature*. Translated by Samuel I. Stone. New York: George Braziller, Inc., 1959.

Mauriac, François, *"Le Bloc-Notes de François Mauriac."* *L'Express*, December 3, 1959, 44.

Ménard, René, *"Antonin Artaud et la condition poétique."* *Critique*, No. 119 (April, 1957), 299–311.

Milne, Tom, "Cruelly, cruelly." *Encore*, No. 48 (March-April, 1964), 9–14.

Monnerot, Jules, *La poésie moderne et le sacré*. Paris: Gallimard, 1949.

Nadeau, Maurice, *Histoire du surréalisme*. 2 vol. Paris: Seuil, 1948.

Nerguy, Claude, and Brenner, Jacques, *"Visites à Antonin Artaud."* *Cahiers de la Pléiade*, Spring, 1949, 109–113.

Nietzsche, Friedrich, *The Birth of Tragedy and the Genealogy of Morals*. Anchor Book. New York: Doubleday, 1956.

Nin, Anaïs, *Diary of Anaïs Nin, 1931–1934*. New York: Swallow Press & Harcourt, Brace & World, 1966.

———— *Under a Glass Bell*. New York: Dutton, 1948.

Nordmann, Jean-Gabriel, *"Antonin Artaud et le surréalisme."* *Europe*, No. 475–476 (November-December, 1968), 153–161.

Paz, Octavio, *"André Breton ou la recherche du commencement."* *la Nouvelle Revue Française*, No. 172 (April, 1967), 606–619.

Pichette, Henri, *Lettres Arc-en-ciel*. Paris: l'Arche, 1950.

Picon, Gaëtan, *L'Usage de la lecture*. II. Paris: Mercure de France, 1961.

Poulet, Robert *Aveux spontanés*. Paris: Plon, 1963.

———— *La lanterne magique*. Paris: Debresse, 1956.

Prabhavananda, Swami, and Manchester, Frederick, *The Spiritual Heritage of India*. Anchor Book. New York: Doubleday, 1964.

Prével, Jacques, *"En compagnie d'Artaud."* *la Nouvelle Revue Fran-*

çaise, No. 110 (February, 1962), 378–388; No. 111 (March, 1962), 578–584.

Rollin, Jean-François, *"Artaud poète de la chair." Strophes,* No. 4 (November, 1964), 57-61.

Rousseaux, André, *Littérature du 20ieme siècle.* Vol. VI. Paris: Albin Michel, 1958.

Rousselot, Jean, *Présences contemporaines.* Paris: Debresse, 1958.

Roy, Claude, *"Le théâtre de la cruauté en Europe." la Nouvelle Revue Française,* No. 149 (May 1, 1965), 895–903.

Saillet, Maurice, *Billets doux de Justin Saget.* Paris: Mercure de France, 1952.

———. *Sur la route de Narcisse.* Paris: Mercure de France, 1958.

"Saint Artaud." *Times Literary Supplement* (London), March 18, 1965, 214.

Scholem, Gershom, *Major Trends in Jewish Mysticism.* New York: Schocken, 1961.

Scott, Nathan, *Samuel Beckett.* London: Bowes & Bowes, 1965.

Seligman, Kurt, *The History of Magic.* New York: Pantheon, 1948.

Sellin, Eric, *The Dramatic Concepts of Antonin Artaud.* University of Chicago Press, 1968.

——— "Antonin Artaud and an Objectified Language of the Stage." *Esprit Créateur,* VI, No. 1 (Spring, 1966), 31–36.

Seymour, Alan, "Artaud's Cruelty." *London Magazine,* III, No. 12 (March, 1964), 59–64.

Sollers, Philippe, *"La pensée émet des signes." Tel Quel,* No. 20 (Winter, 1965), 12–26.

Sontag, Susan, *Against Interpretation.* Delta Book. New York: Dell, 1967.

Steiner, George, *Language and Silence.* New York: Atheneum, 1967.

Thévenin, Paule, "Letter on Artaud." *Tulane Drama Review,* IX, No. 3 (Spring, 1965), 99–117.

——— *"Lettre." Les Lettres Nouvelles,* No. 41 (September, 1956), 363–367.

——— *"Entendre/Voir/Lire." Tel Quel,* No. 39 (Autumn, 1969), 31–63; No. 40 (Winter, 1970), 67–99.

Thomas, Henri, *"Le point mort." Cahiers de la Pléiade,* Spring, 1948, 15–18.

——— *"Le théâtre mort et vivant." l'Heure nouvelle,* No. 1 (1946), 45–50.

Tibetan Book of the Dead. Edited by W. Y. Evans-Wentz. Galaxy Book. New York: Oxford University Press, 1960.

Touly, M., *Entretiens psychiatriques.* No. 11. Toulouse: Edouard Privat, 1965.

La Tour de Feu, No. 63–64 (December, 1959). Issue entitled *"Antonin Artaud ou la santé des poètes."*

———— No. 69 (April, 1961). Issue entitled *"De la contradiction au sommet."*

Tournay, Jean, *"Antonin Artaud: l'exigence de la déraison." Synthèses,* No. 254–255 (August-September, 1967), 66–70.

Tulane Drama Review, VIII, No. 2 (Winter, 1963) .

Tzara, Tristan, *"Antonin Artaud et le désespoir de la connaissance." Les Lettres Françaises,* No. 201 (March 25, 1948), 1–2.

The Upanishads. Edited by Swami Nikhilananda. Harper Torchbook. New York: Harper & Row, 1964.

Virmaux, Alain, "Artaud and Film." *Tulane Drama Review,* XI, No. 1 (Fall, 1966), 154–165.

Vygotsky, Lev Semenovich, *Thought and Language.* Cambridge: MIT Press, 1962.

Wellwarth, George, *The Theater of Protest and Paradox.* New York University Press, 1964.

Zeller, Eduard, *Outlines of the History of Greek Philosophy.* New York: Meridian, 1955.

Zorilla, Oscar, *Antonin Artaud: Una metafísica de la escena.* Mexico: Instituto Nacional de Bellas Artes, 1967.

INDEX